SAP Basis from Zero to Hero

SAP Basis from Zero to Hero

Rezza Prayogi

Zico Pratama Putra

Kanzul Ilmi Press

2017

First Printing: 2017

ISBN: 978-1-521-15827-2

Kanzul Ilmi Press
Woodside Ave.
London, UK

Bookstores and wholesalers: Please contact Kanzul Ilmi Press
email: zico.pratama@gmail.com
Trademark Acknowledgments

All terms mentioned in this book that are known to be trademarks or service marks have been appropriately capitalized. SAP SE, cannot attest to the accuracy of this information. Use of a term in this book should not be regarded as affecting the validity of any trademark or service mark.

SAP Basis is registered trademark of SAP SE.

Unless otherwise indicated herein, any third-party trademarks that may appear in this work are the property of their respective owners and any references to third party trademark, logos or other trade dress are for demonstrative or descriptive purposes only

Ordering Information:
Special discounts are available on quantity purchases by corporations, associations, educators, and others. For details, contact the publisher at the above listed address.

Contents

Introduction

Hello and welcome to SAP Basis from Zero to Hero. This is a fast and effective beginner's computer course, and assumes that you have no experience with SAP. In this course, you'll learn how to install SAP, use or working with SAP, configure SAP, so that you can bring your computer skills to the next level, and put yourself ahead of the competition.

What is SAP R/3?

SAP stands for **Systems Applications and Products in Data Processing**. It was founded in 1972 by Wellenreuther, Hopp, Hector, Plattner and Tschira.

SAP commands unparalleled premium in the ERP & IT market. SAP has the largest market share of all ERP systems. If you are new, we recommend you refer the tutorials sequentially one after the other.

SAP Basis is the heart of a SAP installation and is set of middleware programs and tools which connect all modules in SAP.

Course Requisites

Nothing! This course assumes you an absolute beginner to SAP.

What software do I need?

You need SAP R/3 Front End to do this course, and Internet connection. You can install SAP Backend in your PC or using Backend from Internet.

Where do I start?

Use Contents menu. Each link in table contents takes you to a tutorial chapter. There's plenty of screenshots to keep you on track, and exercises to complete to bring your skills along.

Chapter 1. Getting Started with SAP

What is SAP?

SAP stands for **Systems Applications and Products in Data Processing**. It was founded in 1972 by Wellenreuther, Hopp, Hector, Plattner, and Tschira. **SAP is also named of the ERP (Enterprise Resource Planning) software as well the name of the company.**

SAP system comprises of a number of fully integrated modules, which covers virtually every aspect of the business management. SAP is #1 in the ERP market. As of 2010, SAP has more than 140,000 installations worldwide, over 25 industry-specific business solutions and more than 75,000 customers in 120 countries

Other Competitive products in the market are Oracle, Microsoft Dynamics etc.

Why is it required?

The following story will explain the need of ERP software like SAP in an enterprise.

The very basic question is why Enterprise Resource Planning also called ERP is required? To answer this, let us examine this typical business scenario.

Sales Team approaches the Inventory department to check for availability of the product. In case the product is out of stock, the sales team approaches the Production Planning Department to manufacture the product. The Production Planning Team checks with inventory department for availability of raw material

If the raw material is not available with inventory, the Production Planning team buys the raw material from the Vendors then Production Planning forwards the raw materials to the Shop Floor Execution for actual production.

Once ready, the Shop Floor Team forwards the goods to the Sales Team, who in turn deliver it to the client. The Sales Team updates the Finance with revenue generated by sale of product

Production planning Team update the finance with payments to be made to different vendors for raw materials. All departments approach the HR for any Human Resource related issue. That is a typical business process of in a manufacturing company.

Some Key Inferences one could derive from the scenario would be. A typical Enterprise has many Departments or Business Units. These Departments or Business Units continuously communicate and exchange data with each other.

The success of any organization lies in effective communication, and data exchange, within these departments, as well as associated Third Party such as Vendors, Outsourcers, and Customers. Based on the way communication and data exchanged is managed, enterprise systems can be broadly classified as

1) Decentralized System.
2) Centralized System which is also called as ERP.

Let us look at Decentralized system first. In a company with Decentralized System of Data Management - Data is maintained locally at the individual departments; Departments do not have access to information or data of other Departments

To identify problems arising due to decentralized Enterprise management system lets look at the same business process again. The Customer approaches the sales team for a product, but this time around he needs the product, on an urgent basis. The Sales Team do not have real-time information access to the products inventory.

So, they approach the Inventory department to check the availability of the product. This process takes time and customer chooses another vendor

Loss of Revenue and Customer Dissatisfaction.

Now, suppose the product is out of stock and the Sales Team approaches the Production Planning team to manufacture the product for future use.

Production Planning Team checks the availability of the raw materials required.

Raw Material Information is separately stored by Production Planning as well as Inventory Department.

Thus, Data Maintenance Cost (in this case Raw Material) goes up.

A raw material required to manufacture the product is available in the inventory, but as per the database of the production planning team, the raw material is out of stock.

So, they go ahead and buy the raw material. Thus, material as well inventory cost goes up. Once the raw material is available, the shop floor department suddenly realize they are short of workers

They approach the HR, who in turn hire temporary employees at higher than market rates. Thus, labor cost increases. The production planning department fails to update the finance department on the materials they have purchased.

The finance department defaults the payment deadline set by the vendor causing the company loss of its reputation and even inviting a possible legal action. This is just a few of many a problem with decentralized systems.

Some major problems with the decentralized system are:
- many disparate information systems are developed individually over time which is difficult to maintain.
- Integrating the data is time and money consuming
- Inconsistencies and duplication of data
- Lack of timely information leads to customer dissatisfaction, loss of revenue and repute high Inventory, material and human resource cost.

These are some major drawbacks for which we need a solution. Well the Solution lies in centralized systems i.e. ERP.

In a company, with centralized system of information and data management:
1) Data is maintained at a central location and is shared with various Departments.
2) Departments have access to information or data of other Departments.

Let us look at the same business process again to understand how a centralized enterprise system helps to overcome problems posed by a decentralized enterprise system. In this Case, all departments update a Central Information System when customer approaches the sales team to buy a product on an urgent basis

The Sales Team has real-time information access to the products in inventory which is updated by the Inventory Department in the Centralized System. Sales Team respond on time leading to

Increased Revenue and Customer Delight. In case, manufacturing is required, the Sales Team updates the Centralized Database.

Production Planning Department is auto updated by the Centralized Database for requirements. Production Planning Team checks the availability of the raw materials required via Central Database which is updated by the Inventory Department. Thus, Data Duplication is avoided and accurate data is made available

The Shop Floor Team updates their Man Power Status regularly in the Central Database which can be accessed by the HR department. In the case of shortage of workforce, the HR team starts the recruitment process with considerable lead time to hire a suitable candidate at market price. Thus, labor cost goes down

Vendors can directly submit their invoices to the Central Enterprise System which can be accessed by the Finance Department. Thus, payments are made on time and possible legal actions are avoided

The key benefits of the centralized system are:

- It eliminates the duplication, discontinuity, and redundancy in data
- Provides information across departments in real time.
- Provides control over various business processes
- Increases productivity, better inventory management, promotes quality, reduced material cost, effective human resources management, reduced overheads boosts profits
- Better Customer Interaction, increased throughput. Improves Customer Service
- Hence, a Centralized Enterprise Management System is required.
- SAP is a Centralized Enterprise Management System also known as Enterprise Resource Planning.

SAP Business Suite

Most people relate SAP with its ERP offering. But SAP now offers a variety of products to address varied needs of an organization. Let's have a look at them:

- **SAP HANA**: High-Performance Analytic Appliance uses in-memory computing, a breakthrough technology that enables analysis of very large, non-aggregated data at unprecedented speed in local memory (vs. disk-based database) enabling complex analyses, plans and simulations on real-time data.

- **SAP Convergent Charging**: SAP Convergent Charging provides a rating and charging solution for high-volume processing in service industries. It delivers pricing design capabilities, high-performance rating, and convergent balance management.

- **Customer Relationship Management:** Unlike other CRM software, the SAP Customer Relationship Management (SAP CRM) application, part of the SAP Business Suite, not only helps you address your short-term imperatives – to reduce cost and increase your decision-making ability – but can also help your company achieve differentiated capabilities to compete effectively over the long term.

- **Enterprise Resource Planning:** A sound foundation is necessary to compete and win in the global marketplace. The SAP ERP applications support the essential functions of your business processes and operations efficiently and are tailored to specific needs of your industry like SAP ERP Financials, SAP ERP Human capital management, SAP ERP Operations, SAP ERP corporate services.

- **SAP Environment, Health, and Safety Management**: It supports environmental, occupational and product safety processes, regulatory compliance, and corporate responsibility. This is accomplished by embedding corporate policies, compliance, and environmental, health and safety capabilities with global business processes for human resources, logistics, production, and finance.

- **SAP Global Batch Traceability:** It allows you to completely trace tracked objects, for example, a batch, across both SAP systems and non-SAP systems. In the event of a recall or withdrawal, SAP GBT ensures the timely compliance with legal reporting timelines. Furthermore, it helps you to minimize cost and corporate risk exposure. You can also analyze multiple objects, for example, batches, in one run.

- **SAP Product Life Cycle Management:** To survive in an ever-changing global environment, creating and delivering innovative and market differentiating products and services is what distinguishes your company from the competition. The SAP Product Lifecycle Management (SAP PLM) application provides you with a 360-degree-support for all product-related processes – from the first product idea, through manufacturing to product service

- **SAP Supplier Life Cycle Management:** SAP Supplier Lifecycle Management is a holistic approach to managing supplier relationships. It deals with the supply base to constantly determine the right mix of suppliers. It covers the lifecycle of individual supplier's – from on boarding to a continuous development.

- **Supply Chain Management**: You face enormous pressure to reduce costs while increasing innovation and improving customer service and responsiveness. SAP Supply Chain Management (SAP SCM) enables collaboration, planning, execution, and coordination of the entire supply network, empowering you to adapt your supply chain processes to an ever-changing competitive environment.

- **Supplier Relationship Management**: With SAP SRM you can examine and forecast purchasing behavior, shorten procurement cycles, and work with your partners in real time. This allows you to develop long-term relationships with all those suppliers that have proven themselves to be reliable partners.

- **Governance, Risk, and Compliance:** Risk is unavoidable, but it can be managed. With governance, risk, and compliance (GRC), businesses can strategically balance risk and opportunity.

- **Sales and operations planning:** SAP Sales and Operations Planning enables you to optimally and profitably meet long-term future demand. Typically, this process repeats every month and involves many participants including Sales, Marketing, Finance, Demand Planning, and Supply Chain Planning.

- **SAP Transportation Management**: It supports you in all activities connected with the physical transportation of goods from one location to another.

- **Extended Warehouse Management:** SAP Extended Warehouse Management gives you the option of mapping your entire warehouse complex in detail in the system, down to the storage bin level. Not only does this give you an overview of the total quantity of a product in the warehouse, but you can also always see exactly where a specific product is, at any time, in your warehouse complex. With EWM, you can optimize the use of various storage bins and stock movements and then combine the storage of stocks from several plants in randomly-managed warehouses.

- **Mobile Apps**: Mobile devices can also access SAP system.

SAP Modules

A SAP system is divided into modules like MM, SD which maps business process of that department or business unit.

Following is the list of module available in SAP system.

1. **SAP FI Module**- FI stands for Financial Accounting
2. **SAP CO Module**- CO stands for Controlling
3. **SAP PS Module** - and PS is Project Systems
4. **SAP HR Module** - HR stands for Human Resources
5. **SAP PM Module** - where Plant Maintenance is the PM
6. **SAP MM Module** - MM is Materials Management -
7. **SAP QM Module** - QM stands for Quality Management
8. **SAP PP Module** - PP is Production Planning
9. **SAP SD Module** - SD is Sales and Distribution
10. **SAP BW Module** - where BW stands for Business (Data) Warehouse
11. **SAP EC Module** - where EC stands for Enterprise Controlling
12. **SAP TR Module** - where TR stands for Treasury
13. **SAP IM Module** - where IM stands for Investment Management
14. **SAP - IS** where IS stands for Industries specific solution
15. **SAP - Basis**
16. **SAP - ABAP**
17. **SAP - Cross Application Components**
18. **SAP - CRM** where CRM stands for Customer Relationship Management
19. **SAP - SCM** where SCM stands for Supply Chain Management
20. **SAP - PLM** where PLM stands for Product LiveCycle Management
21. **SAP - SRM** where SRM stands for Supplier Relationship Management
22. **SAP - CS** where CS stands for Customer Service

23. **SAP - SEM** where SEM stands for STRATEGIC ENTERPRISE MANAGEMENT
24. **SAP - RE** where RE stands for Real Estate

Why SAP is divided into Modules

SAP is divided into Modules because of:

- One of the principle reasons why **SAP is so popular is that it is very flexible and customizable.** It is said that if you have the time and money you can make SAP software to drive your car on autopilot

- **One way to achieve this flexibility is to break SAP system into different Modules like HR, Finance and so on which emulate business processes of that department or Business Unit**

- You can integrate one module with other or even third party interfaces.

- Now depending upon your organization, you can have just module, or a few, or all the modules of SAP implemented. Also, you can have integration with Third Party Systems

- It is also possible to integrate modules from different ERP Vendors. So, you can integrate

- PP Module from SAP, with HR Module of PeopleSoft

- The various SAP Modules available are

- Financial Modules like Financial Accounting, Controlling etc.

- Logistics Modules like Materials, Sales etc.

- Human Resource Management Modules. Human Resource Module will emulate HR related business processes like hiring, appraisals, termination etc.

- Likewise, Financial Accounting which will emulate Finance related business processes and manage financial data likewise

- Cross Application Modules, which essentially integrate SAP with other software applications

- For our learning purposes let's focus on SAP HR module. SAP- HR provides comprehensive business processes, which map all HR activities in an enterprise.

- The various sub modules or functionalities supported by SAP - HR is Recruitment
- Training & Development, Time Management, Employee Benefits, Payroll, Travel
- Cost Planning, Reporting, ESS & MSS
- We will consider the details of the sub-modules later in the trainings

What is mySAP?

mySAP is **not a single product but is a suite of products from SAP including SAP R/3.**

SAP R/3 was first launched in 1998, is regularly updated, and is market leader in ERP category till date.

SAP R/3 many modules such as HR, Finance, MM covering all enterprise   Functions

"3" stands for three tier architecture - Presentation tier, Logic tier and Data tier.

Other product in the mySAP product suite includes SRM (Supplier Relationship Management), CRM (Customer Relationship Management), PLM (Product Lifecycle Management), and SCM (Supply Chain Management).

What is NetWeaver?

NetWeaver is SAP's **integrated technology platform, and is not a product.** In fact, new version of basis is called the NetWeaver.

It is the underlying technology for all the products in the mySAP suite.

All the products in mySAP suite can run on a single instance of NetWeaver's, SAP Web Application Server, also known as "SAP WEBAs"

NetWeaver makes possible access of SAP data using simple http protocol or even mobile. This eliminates the need of installing and more importantly training in SAP's client side software.

The core capabilities of SAP NetWeaver are the integration of people, information, and process.

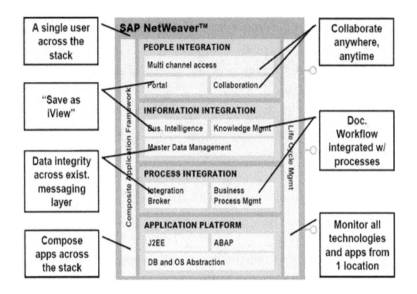

People integration

It simply means that it enables you to bring people together and help them work more efficiently.

Examples:

- **Portal:** provides industry leading portal technology that delivers unified, personalized, and role-based user access
- **Collaboration:** Collaboration promotes cooperation in enterprises using virtual team rooms (Collaboration Rooms), real-time communication (chat and application sharing) and the use of third-party groupware and synchronous collaboration tools (for example, Microsoft Exchange, Lotus Notes, and WebEx)
- **Multi-Channel Access:** With Multi-Channel Access, you can connect to enterprise systems through web-based, voice, mobile, messaging, or radio-frequency technology.

Information integration

It means you can bring together information from a variety of locations and have it make sense in the context of what your folks do every day! **Examples:**

- **Business Intelligence**: It provides you with reliable tools for creating individual and interactive reports and applications.
- **BI Content & BI Content Extensions**: Enables quicker implementation using pre-configured role and task oriented information models in SAP Business Intelligence.
- **Knowledge Management**: Allows common access to unstructured information and documents in a distributed storage landscape like **Search, Classification, Subscription, Versioning, etc.**
- **Search and Classification (TREX):** Provides SAP applications with numerous services for searching, classifying, and text-mining in large collections of documents (unstructured data) as well as for searching in and aggregating business objects (structured data).

Process integration

It means coordinating the flow of work across departments, divisions, and between companies. Usage type process integration includes all functions previously covered by SAP NetWeaver Exchange Infrastructure that you use to realize cross-system business processes. This SAP NetWeaver usage type enables different versions of SAP and non-SAP systems from different vendors running on different platforms (for example, Java ABAP, and so on) to communicate with each other. SAP NetWeaver is based on an open architecture, primarily uses open standards (those from the XML and Java environments), and provides services that are essential in a heterogeneous and complex system landscape. These include a runtime infrastructure for exchanging messages, configuration options for managing business processes and the flow of messages, as well as options for mapping messages before they reach the receiver.

Application Platform

SAP Web Application Server provides a complete development infrastructure on which you can develop, distribute, and execute platform-independent, robust, and scalable Web services and business applications. SAP Web Application Server supports ABAP, Java, and Web services.

SAP GUI and Navigation

This training material will help you understand SAP GUI in greater detail as well as learn its navigational structure.

When you logon to SAP or you open a new session, you will see the following screen

Let's look into the various screen elements.

SAP User Menu

The SAP User Menu is tailored to the user's specific needs. It includes all transactions relevant to a user, grouped under relevant folders.

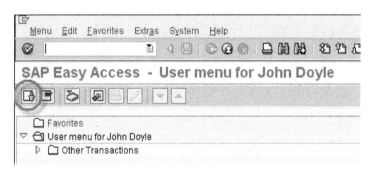

SAP Easy Access Menu

The SAP Easy Access Menu includes all transactions offered by SAP, grouped in folders according to SAP modules (FI/CO, MM, etc.). It is not tailored to the user's specific needs.

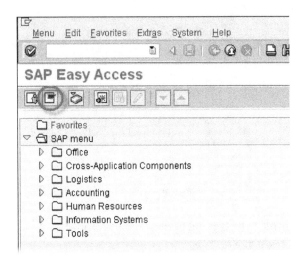

SAP Menu Bar

The SAP Menu Bar CHANGES from one screen to another. You follow a menu path to access a function or a transaction.

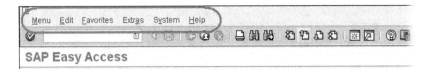

SAP Standard Tool Bar

The SAP Standard Toolbar does **NOT** change from one transaction to another. You can use the SAP Standard Toolbar to execute various functions.

- Buttons available are enabled
- Buttons not available are disabled
- In the "Transaction Box", you can directly access a transaction, without using the SAP Menu, by entering the transaction code

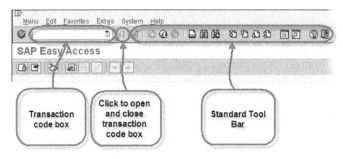

General Icons and their Description

Back	Information Status
Exit	Tab List
Cancel	Print
Enter	Execute
Save	User menu
Search	open a session

Hint: You open a maximum of 6 different SAP sessions at a time

SAP Application Toolbar

The SAP Application Toolbar CHANGES from one screen to another.

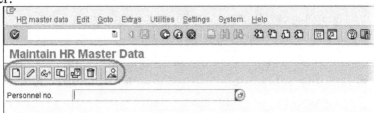

SAP Status Bar

The SAP Status Bar does NOT change from one screen to another. It tells you WHERE you are in SAP:

- Which environment you are using (Production, Development, Quality).
- In which session you are in (as you can open up to 6 sessions).
- What client you are using.

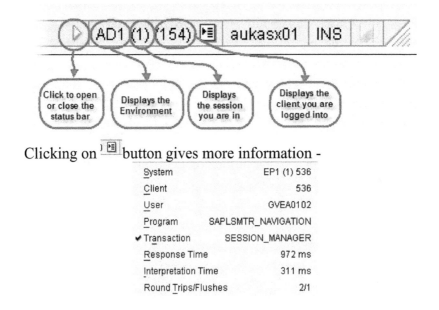

Clicking on ⃞ button gives more information -

System	EP1 (1) 536
Client	536
User	GVEA0102
Program	SAPLSMTR_NAVIGATION
✔ Transaction	SESSION_MANAGER
Response Time	972 ms
Interpretation Time	311 ms
Round Trips/Flushes	2/1

SAP Function Keys

Functions keys are just another way of navigating around SAP. The availability of function keys **CHANGES** from one screen to another While in a transaction, right click on your mouse, you will see a list of function keys available

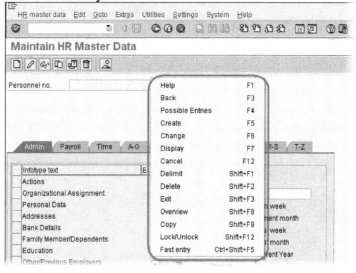

Chapter 2. Introduction to SAP Basis

What is BASIS?

The full form of BASIS is **"Business Application Software Integrated solution"**. Basis is a set of programs and tools that act as an interface with Database, Operating System, Communication protocols and business applications (such as FI, CO, MM, etc.).

SAP applications such as FI, CO, PP etc. can run and communicate with each other across different Operating systems and Databases with the help of BASIS.

Nowadays Basis is known as **NetWeaver**.

Alias of BASIS is SAP Application Server Technology and alias of NetWeaver is SAP Web Application Server.

After adding **java stack (the applications which are developed in J2EE, BSP, JSP, etc..), enhanced security standard for business process.** Both ABAP and Java stack can be monitored from one platform. NetWeaver supports standard protocols such as HTTP, SMTP, XML, SOAP, SSO, WEBDAV, WSDL, WMLSSO, SSL, X.509 and Unicode format **(representation of handling text)**.

We can say **Basis is the operating system for SAP applications and ABAP.** Basis provides services like communication with the operating system, database communication, memory management, runtime collection of application data, web requests, exchanging business data etc.

Basis supports many of known operating systems (Unix flavors, Microsoft windows server edition, AS400, z/OS, etc.) and databases (Oracle, DB2, Informix, Maxdb, Microsoft SQL Server, etc.).

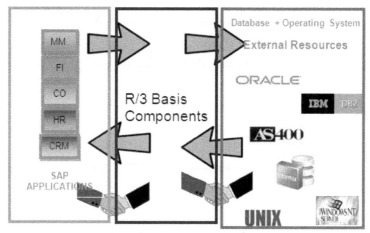

As we know **BASIS** is a set of tools. This tool has the following different functionalities:

- System monitoring and administration tools
- Common monitoring tool CCMS (**Computing Center Management System**) to monitor alerts of R/3 system from a one place.
- Server side scripting in ABAP and JavaScript.
- Use of Business server pages to build online stores and portals.
- Database monitoring and administration utilities
- Resource management like memory, buffer, etc.
- Authorization and profile management tools for user management.
- Internet access control to the system and business objects.
- Transfer modifications in screen, program, and layout from the development to production system for accuracy purpose by **Transport Management System.**
- Client server architecture and configuration.
- Graphical User Interface designing for the presentation layer.

SAP Basis consultant's responsibilities

SAP Basis is a middleware tool for applications, operating system and database. SAP Basis consultant should able to do the following tasks:

- SAP application server monitoring, ABAP dump and system log analysis.
- Performance tuning
- Database maintenance, Database backup schedule and restore
- R/3, NetWeaver, solution manager installation, etc.
- SAP license maintenance.
- SAP landscape, transport management system installations, etc.
- Client creating, client copying, client deletion, etc.
- Creating user, assigning roles, locking and unlocking users, etc.
- Background jobs scheduling, job monitoring, job deletion, etc.
- Profile and operation mode maintenance
- Applying support patches, upgrading and installing add-ons
- SNOTE applying and removing errors.
- System copy, System refresh, etc.

These are generic list. There are many other responsibilities that a Basis consultant shoulders. Every day you learn something new!

Install SAP GUI (Front End)

Before you can configure and use the SAP GUI, you need to download the software from the SAP Marketplace as per steps below:

Step 1) Go to service.sap.com

Step 2) Enter S-user and password as provided by SAP.

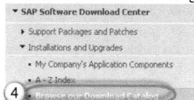

Step 3) Go to "Software Downloads"

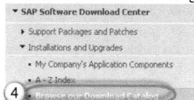

Step 4) Choose "Browse our download Catalog"

Step 5) Choose SAP Frontend component.

Analytics Solutions
> like Address Directories & Reference Data, Crystal Reports Viewer, SBOP Data Federator, SBOP Enterprise, SBOP Extended Analytics, SBOP Text Analysis, ...

SAP Business One
> like SAP Business One 8.8, SAP Business One 2007, Crystal Reports for B1, Remote Support Platform for B1, ...

SAP Connectors
> like Business Connector, ...

SAP Content
> like B1 CONT, SAP Business ByDesign CONTENT, ...

SAP Cryptographic Software
> like SAP Cryptographic Library, ...

SAP Development Projects
> like customer-specific development projects software, ...

SAP Education Products
> like Acrobat Con Learning by Adobe, Knowledge Acceleration, RWD Info Pak Suite—SAP

SAP Frontend Components   (5)
> like NetWeaver Business Client, SAP GUI for Windows, SAP GUI for JAVA, SAP ITS, SAP IGS, ...

SAP In-Memory (SAP HANA)
> like SAP HANA Enterprise Edition, SAP HANA Enterprise Ext. Edit., SAP HANA Platform Edition

SAP Mobile Solutions
> like MOB ACCAPROVER INT, MOB HR APPROVAL INT, MOB MGR INSIGHT IPD, ...

SAP NetWeaver and complementary products
> like SAP NetWeaver, SAP NetWeaver CE, SAP NetWeaver Mobile, SAP NW Identity Management, SAP MDM, SAP Content Server, ...

SAP On-Demand Solutions
> like SAP Sales OD Integration

SAP Rapid Deployment solutions
> like SAP Business Communication Management rapid-deployment solution, SAP CRM rapid-deployment solution for Sales, Marketing, and Service, SAP IT Service Desk Operation rapid-deployment solution, ...

Step 6) Choose SAP GUI for your OS. In this demo, we will select Windows

SAP FRONTEND COMPONENTS   Ca

- NETWEAVER BUSINESS CLIENT   • SAP GUI FOR JAVA
- SAP DATA PANEL FOR MS WORD   • SAP IGS
(6) SAP GUI FOR WINDOWS

Step 7) Choose SAP GUI 7.30 Core which is the latest one.

Step 8) Choose installation

Step 9) Choose Add to download Basket

Step 10) Choose the Download Basket

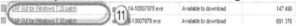

Step 11) Choose your download and it will begin.

Time to configure your GUI

Once the download is complete and you have installed the software, it's time to configure it:
Step 1) Click on create button as shown below.

Step 2) Click next button

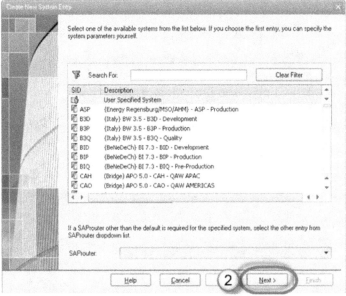

Step 3) Fill the Server details
1. **Connection Type**: Custom Application Server (One host)
2. **Description**: Name of instance
3. **Application Server**: IP address of remote application server
4. **Instance number** which you can find from OS level (Unix)

Go to /usr/sap/sid/DVEBGMS00 Here instance number = 00

System ID: As per you setting which you have specified during installation time.

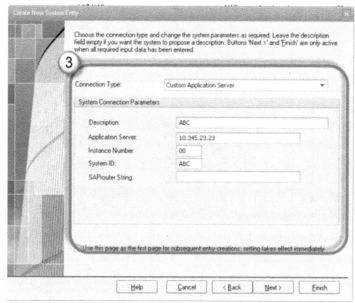

Step 4) Created system will be there in the list as per shown below.

Double Click on the instance to log-in to a SAP Server.

What is SAP Instance & SID?

What is an Instance?

An SAP R/3 instance defines a group of resources such as

- memory
- work processes
- dispatcher
- gateway

Usually for a single application or database server within an SAP R/3 client-server environment.

Basically, there are three types of instances:

1. Dialog instance
2. Central Instance
3. Database Instance

SAP System = Dialog Instance + Central Instance + Database Instance.

For one SAP system, all three instances share the same directory.

- **Dialog Instance**: Dialog instance exists in the application layer. Its purpose is to maintain load on the server. Dialog instance exists on different host. If number of dialog instance increases hardware resources, dispatcher, work processes also increases so that more number of users can login at a time.

- **Central Instance**: Central instance can also work as dialog instance. But the main thing is that it contains enqueue and message servers. All dialog instances communicate with central instance before requesting database with message server. When an instance is started, the dispatcher process attempts to establish a connection to the message server so that it can announce the services it provides (DIA, BTC, SPO, UPD, etc.). Lock table is managed in central instance by enqueue service.

- **Database Instance**: As normal database instance accepts requests from central instance to fulfil the user's requests. As lock management system provided by enqueue server it will provide service to users.

What is SID?

Each R/3 installation (SAP system) of a database server and several app servers running the application logic is uniquely identified by a single SID (SAP System Identification), SAPSID — a three-character code such as C11, PRD, E56, etc.),

Logical System Names:
When data is distributed between different systems, each system within a network should be clearly identifiable. The "logical system" deals with this issue.

A logical system is an application system in which the applications work together on a common database. In SAP terms, the logical system is a client.

Since the logical system name is used to identify a system uniquely within the network, two systems cannot have the same name if they are connected to each other as BW systems or as source systems, or if there are plans to connect them in any way.

Example for production system logical system name might be:
SID – PBG
SID Description - P=Production(type), B=BW(component), G=Germany. (plant name)
Logical System name:
PBGCLNT100.This form is easy to understand.

Introduction to R/3 client-server technology

SAP R/3 uses three-tier architecture.

- **R** signifies Real-time system
- **3** represents - 3-tier architecture.

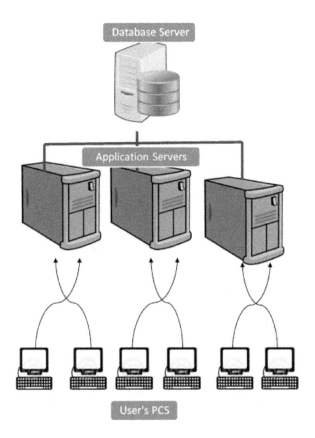

User's PC: Users can access SAP system in two ways:

1. Through SAP GUI
2. Through Web browser

It's called front-end. Only the front-end is installed in the user's PC not the application/database servers.

Front-end takes the user's requests to database server and application servers.

Application Servers: Application server is built to process business-logic. This workload is distributed among multiple application servers. With multiple applications server's, user can get the output more quickly.

Application server exists at a remote location as compared to location of the user PC.

Database Server: Database server stores and retrieves data as per SQL queries generated by ABAP and java applications.

Database and Application may exist on the same or different physical location.

Understanding different SAP layers

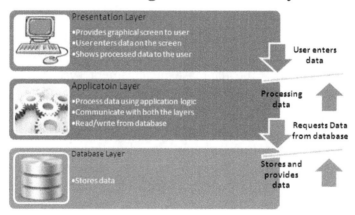

Presentation Layer:

The Presentation Layer contains the software components that make up the SAP GUI (graphical user interface). This layer is the interface between the R/3 System and its users. The R/3 System uses the SAP GUI to provide an intuitive graphical user interface for entering and displaying data.

The presentation layer sends the user's input to the application server, and receives data for display from it. While a SAP GUI component is running, it remains linked to a user's terminal session in the R/3 System.

Application Layer:

The Application Layer consists of one or more application servers and a message server. Each application server contains a set of services used to run the R/3 System. Theoretically, you only need one application server to run an R/3 System. In practice, the services are distributed across more than one application server. The message server is responsible for communication between the application servers. It passes requests from one application server to another within the system. It also contains information about application server groups and the current load balancing within them. It uses this information to assign an appropriate server when a user logs onto the system.

Database Layer:

The Database Layer consists of a central database system containing all the data in the R/3 System. The database system has two components - the database management system (DBMS), and the database itself. SAP has manufactured its own database named HANA but is compatible with all major databases such as Oracle. All R/3 data is stored in the database. For example, the database contains the control and customizing data that determine how your R/3 System runs. It also contains the program code for your applications. Applications consist of program code, screen definitions, menus, function modules, and various other components. These are stored in a special section of the database called the R/3 Repository, and are accordingly called repository objects. R/3 repository objects are used in ABAP workbench.

Understanding the components of SAP R/3 3-tier Architecture

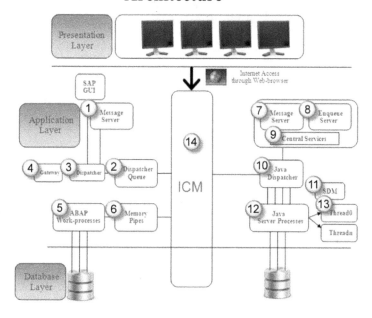

ABAP + Java System Architecture

1. **Message Server: It** handles communication between distributed Dispatchers in ABAP system.
2. **Dispatcher Queue:** Various work process types are stored in this queue.
3. **Dispatcher:** It distributes requests to the work processes.
4. **Gateway:** It enables communication between SAP system and between SAP system and external systems.
5. **ABAP-Work processes:** It separately executes dialog steps in R/3 applications.

Types of work processes are given as below:

Dialog	• Responsible for dialog process
Update	• Responsible for update
Update2	• Responsible for less time critical update
Background	• Responsible for background job
Spool	• Responsible for outpur requests
Enqueue	• Responsible for locks

6. **Memory-pipes:** It enables communication between ICM and ABAP work processes.
7. **Message Server:** It handles java dispatchers and server processes. It enables communication within java runtime environment.
8. **Enqueue Server:** It handles logical locks that are set by the executed Java application program in a server process.
9. **Central Services:** Java cluster requires a special instance of the central services for managing locks and transmitting messages and data. Java cluster is a set of processes that work together to build reliable system. Instance is group of resources such as memory, work processes and so on.
10. **Java Dispatcher:** It receives the client requests and forwards to the server process.
11. **SDM:** Software Deployment Manager is used to install J2EE components.
12. **Java Server Processes:** It can process many requests simultaneously.
13. **Threading:** Multiple Processes executes separately in the background; this concept is called threading.
14. **ICM:** It enables communication between SAP system and HTTP, HTTPS, SMTP protocol. It means by entering system URL in the browser you can access SAP from browser also.

One more component is JCO. JCO is used to handle communication between java dispatcher and ABAP dispatcher when system is configured as ABAP + Java.

How the SAP Logon Process works?

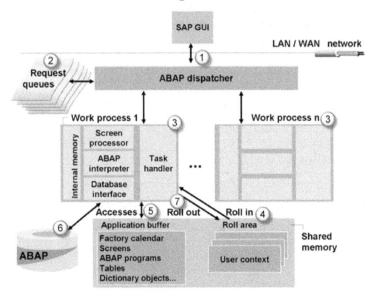

Step 1) Once user click on the SAP system from GUI, User request is forwarded to **Dispatcher.**

Step 2) Request is stored in **Request queues first.** Dispatcher follows **First in First out** rule. It will find free work process and if available will be assigned.

Step 3) As per user request, work process is assigned to user. For example, when user login to the system then Dialog work process is assigned to the user. If user runs a report in background, then background work process is assigned to the user. When some modifications are done at database level then update work process is assigned. So as per user's action work process is assigned.

Step 4) Once user is assigned the dialog work process then user authorizations, user's current setting are rolled in to work-process in shared memory to access user's data. Once dialog step is executed then user's data is rolled out from work process. Thus, shared memory will be cleaned and other user's data can be saved in shared memory area. Dialog step means the screen movements. In a transaction, when a user's jumps from one screen to other the process is called a dialog step.

Step 5) First work process will find the data in the buffer. If it finds data in buffer, then there is no need to retrieve data from database. Thus, response time is improved and this process is called hit. If it does not find the data in buffer, then it will find the data in database and this process is called miss. Hit ratio should be always higher than miss ratio. It improves the performance of system.

Step 6) other requested data is queried from the database and once the process is complete, the result is sent back to **GUI via dispatcher.**

Step 7) at the end user's data is removed from shared memory so the memory will be available to other users. This process is called **roll-out.**

Chapter 3. Clients

What is Client & How to Create a New Client in SAP

What is the Client?

The Client is a 'Customer'. We can say that each customer maps to one client. Within one SAP instance, many Clients can be created. No need to install separate software's for each customer. It provides isolation; one client cannot see the data of another client.

SAP Instance

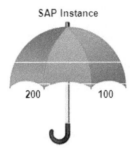

As depicted above 100 and 200 clients exist under one roof. We can create many clients in SAP Application (from 000 to 999)

What does client contain?

1. **Application Data-** Application data is the data that are stored in the database tables.

2. **Customizing Data** - Customizing data is data created by customers when they customize their systems

3. **User Master Record-** A user master record defines the authorizations assigned to a user. Basis consultants are responsible for maintaining the user master record and assigning authorizations

Advantages of Client concept:

1. Clients enable SAP SAS providers to install a small number of SAP Systems, but still cater to a large number of customers.

2. Costs are not only saved by sharing hardware and software but multiple customers also use the same application solution, including administration and support.
3. Clients help establish your SAP landscape. For instance, you can have a client for the development team, a client for a test team and a production client.

SAP comes with three "standard clients":
1. 000
2. 001
3. 066

000 Client: We can find this client in the system as soon as we install SAP r/3 software. This is called master client. Client 000 contains a simple organizational structure of a test company and includes parameters for all applications, standard settings, and configurations for the control of standard transactions and examples to be used in many different profiles of the business applications. It contains client independent data.

001 Client: This client is a copy of the 000 client including the test company. This client's settings are client-independent if it is configured or customized. People normally use 001 clients to create a new client.

066 Client: This client is called early watch client. The SAP early watch alert is a diagnosis service, for solution monitoring of SAP and non-SAP systems in the SAP Solution Manager. Alert may contain Performance issue, average response time, current system load, Database administration, etc.

How to create a new client?

Theoretically we can create clients from 000 to 999. But maintenance of such a large number of clients becomes a challenge.

Step 1) Execute T-Code SCC4

Step 2) it will bring you to the initial screen of SAP clients.

Display View "Clients": Overview

Client	Name	City	Crcy	Changed on
000	SAP AG Konzern	Walldorf	EUR	22.03.2011
066	Test EarlyWatch Profiles	Walldorf	EUR	09.05.2003

Click New Entry to make a new SAP Client

Display View "Clients": Overview

Client	Name	City	Crcy	Changed on
000	SAP AG Konzern	Walldorf	EUR	22.03.2011
066	Test EarlyWatch Profiles	Walldorf	EUR	09.05.2003

Step 3)

1. Enter basic details as given below.
   - Client number & description
   - City to which client Belongs (etc., NY-New York)
   - Logical system may be <SID>CLNT<Client Number>
   - Standard Currency may be (etc. EUR)
   - Client roles may be Customizing, Demo, Training/Education, Production, etc.
2. Enter your client specific data and set permission for the clients as per your requirement
3. Save
4. Press F3 to come back to SCC4

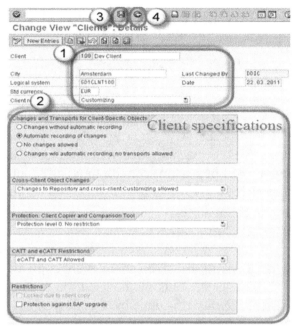

Step 4) New client will be there in the list. Here we have created client 100.

All About Client Copy – Local, Remote, Import/Export

Client Copy

We can generate a blank client with SCC4. *But how to fill the data in the client?" Answer is the client copy."*

Client copy means **"transferring client specific data"** within same instance (SID) or between different instances (SID).

Client copy can be performed with three different methods:

1. Local client copy.
2. Remote client copy.
3. Client Import/Export.

Below brief details are given about client copy methods.

Local Client Copy: This method is used to copy client within the same instance (SID). It is done by T-code **SCCL**.

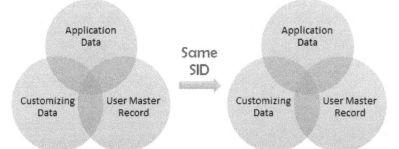

Remote Client Copy: This method is used to copy client between different instances (SID). It is performed by T-code SCC9.

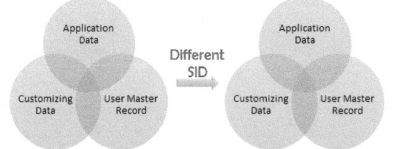

Client Import/Export: This method is used to copy client between different instances (SID). It is performed by T-code **SCC8**

Client Copy Pre-steps

To avoid data inconsistencies there are few pre-steps to be performed before starting client copy:

1) Disconnect and lock business users (SU10). You can end the session of active users in the system through **SM04.** Once all users are logged out, check that no cancelled or pending update requests exist in the system.

2) Suspend all background jobs

- Execute **SE38** as given below.

- Fill program name with "BTCTRNS1" as above figure.
- Press Execute.

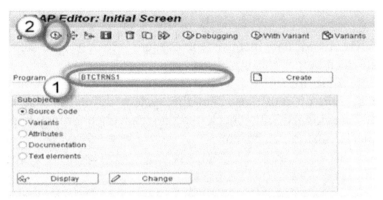

3) **For a local copy, system must have enough space in the database or tablespace.**

For remote copy, target system must have enough space in the database or tablespace. Check space using Tx **DB02.**

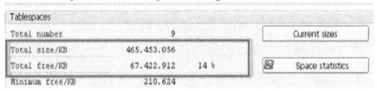

4) To avoid inconsistencies during client copy users should not be allowed to work in source client.

5) **rdisp/max_wprun_time** parameter should be changed to 2000 second as a SAP recommendation. Although you use parallel processes and schedule job in background, dialog processes will be used.

Local Client Copy

Local client copy is performed using **Tcode SCCL**.
Scenario:

- Source Instance & client := **DKM-000**
- Target Instance & client := **DKM-202**

Step 1) Create an entry for your new target client using SCC4. In our scenario, we will create client 202 in DKM system. Log on to this newly created target client (DKM-202) with user SAP* and default password pass.

Step 2) Excute T-code SCCL.

Step 3)

- Select your desired profile
- Enter Source client.
- Enter Description

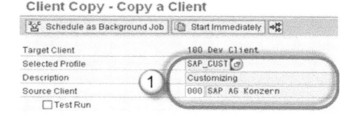

Step 4) By default Client Copy is executed as a single process. Single process will take a lot of time. We will distribute workload of single process to parallel (multiple) processes which will reduce time in copying a client.

1. Select **Go to** from menu bar.

2. Select **Parallel Process**. Parallel processes are used to exploit the capacity of database better

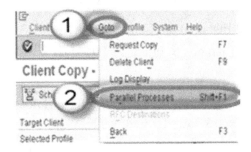

Step 5) Always execute long running processes in background mode rather than foreground/dialog mode. In fact, some processes run more quickly in background.

Step 6) The client copy logs are available in **SCC3**. Status - **"Successfully Completed"** means client copy is completed.

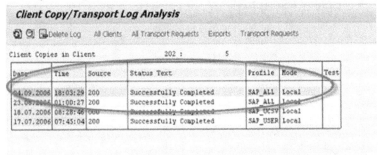

Remote Client Copy

This technique uses Remote function call. You can view RFC from SM59. This technique depends on the network, so network connectivity must be strong enough.

Scenario:

Source Instance & client := **BD1-101**

Target Instance & client := **DKM-202**

Step 1) Log on to the target system. Here we will log on to DKM system. Create a new target client entry (202) using **SCC4**. Log on to this new target client with user **SAP*** and default password "**pass**". Here we will log on to DKM-200 system.

Step 2) Execute Transaction Code SCC9.

Step 3) Fill the basic details as per your requirement.

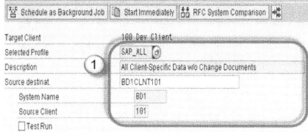

Step 4) Select **Parallel Process**. Parallel processes are used to exploit the capacity of database better.

Step 5) Schedule the client copy in background.

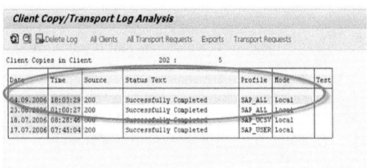

Step 6) The client copy logs are available in SCC3 as given below.

Client Copy/Transport Log Analysis

🔹 🔹 🔹Delete Log   All Clients   All Transport Requests   Exports   Transport Requests

Client Copies in Client   202 :   5

Date	Time	Source	Status Text	Profile	Mode	Test
04.09.2006	18:03:29	200	Successfully Completed	SAP_ALL	Local	
23.08.2006	01:00:27	200	Successfully Completed	SAP_ALL	Local	
18.07.2006	08:28:48	000	Successfully Completed	SAP_UCSV	Local	
17.07.2006	07:45:04	200	Successfully Completed	SAP_USER	Local	

Client Import/Export

For large database, it is recommended to use client import/export instead of remote client copy.
Scenario:
    Source Instance & client := **PKT-300**
    Target Instance & client := **DKM-202**
This technique always starts with client *export* step.

Note: You must have enough space in the /usr/sap/trans_SID file system to perform the client export.

How to export client?

Step 1) Log on to the target system (DKM). Create an entry for your new target client using **SCC4. Log** on to the source system / source client (PKT).

Step 2) Before you import a Client you need to export. Export is nothing but transferring data files and co-files from source system's database to target system's import buffer. Execute T-code **SCC8.**

Step 3)
- Select profile
- Choose target system.

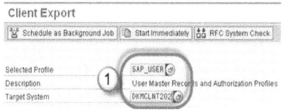

Step 4) Schedule the export in background.

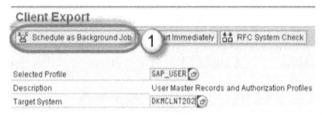

Step 5) Once the job is executed data files and co-files of profiles from **PKT** system's database **are transferred to DKM** system's import buffer. Once we will import request in DKM only then it will be reflected in database of **DKM** system.

Depending on the chosen export profile there can be up to 3 transport requests created:

- Request PKTKO00151 will hold the cross-client data,
- Request PKTKT00151 will hold the client dependent data,
- Request PKTKX00151 will also hold some client dependent data.

How to import the client?

Step 1) Log on to the newly created target client (DKM-202) using SAP* and password pass.

Step 2) Start the **STMS_IMPORT** transaction

As shown below, import queue will open

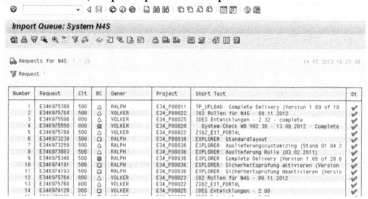

Step 2) Select the transport requests generated by client export. Import theses transport requests on the target client.

The transport requests should be imported in the following sequence:

1. Request PKTKO00151
2. Request PKTKT00151
3. Request PKTKX00151

The system automatically detects these are client export transport requests and automatically performs the import of the 3 requests.

The import logs can be seen in **STMS_IMPORT**.

Step 3) Post import phase:

Once the import is done, execute **SCC7** to perform the post client import actions,

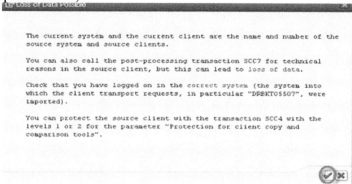

Schedule the post import job in background.

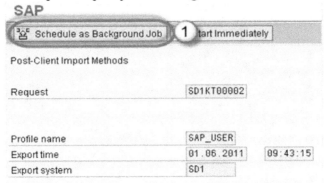

Step 4) Import log will be available in **SCC3.** Client is successfully imported.

How to Delete a Client

Step 1) T-code which is used for client deletion is **SCC5**.

Step 2) Click on "delete in background" to run client deletion as background job. You can also check option **"Delete entry from T000"** table.

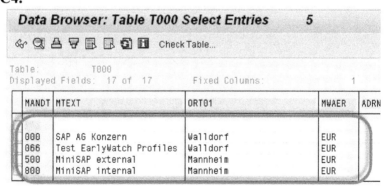

Table "T000" contains clients' entry which we have created in **SCC4**.

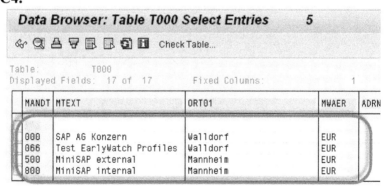

Step 3) Check status of client deletion process using SM50.

Work process overview will open. **"BGD"** denotes background
work process.

10	LNG	12003	Waiting	Yes			
11	BGD	2071	Waiting	Yes			
12	BGD	2094	Waiting	Yes			
13	BGD	1815	Waiting	Yes			
14	BGD	32284	Waiting	Yes			
15	BGD	31109	Running	Yes	8841	SAPLRHAS	800
16	BGD	1766	Waiting	Yes			
17	BGD	1874	Waiting	Yes			
18	BGD	4032	Waiting	Yes			

Once complete. Client will be deleted

Chapter 4. User Authorization

How to Create a SAP User

Step 1) Execute T-code SU01
Step 2)
1. Enter **Username** which you want to create.
2. Click the create button

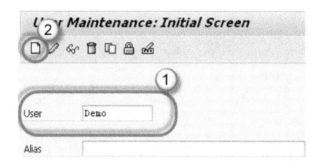

Step 3) In the next screen
1. Click the **Address** tab.
2. Enter Details

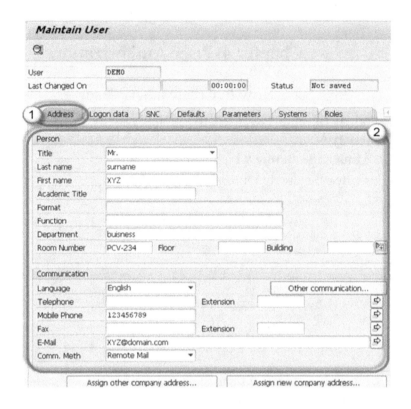

Step 4) Choose the user type in Logon Data tab.

There are 5 types of users in sap: -

1. **Dialog user**: - Normally it is used for interactive system access from GUI (used for human users)
2. **System user**: - Normally it is used for Background processing, communication within a system.
3. **Communication user**: - It is used for external RFC calls.
4. **Service user**: - Dialog user available to a larger, anonymous group of users.
5. **Reference user**: - General, non-person related users that allows the assignment of additional authorizations. Example, Internet users created with transaction SU01. No logon is possible.

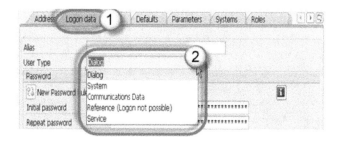

Step 5) Type the **initial password** for 2 times.

On first logon of the new user, system will ask to re-set the password.

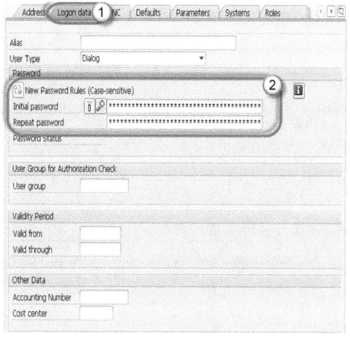

Step 6)
1. Select the roles tab
2. Assign roles as per requirements

Step 7)

1. Select the profiles tab
2. Assign profiles as per requirements

You can assign **SAP_ALL** and **SAP_New** profile to user for **full authorization.**

- **SAP_ALL**: You assign this profile to users who are to have all R/3 authorizations, including super-user authorization.
- **SAP_NEW**: You assign this profile to users who have access to all currently unprotected components. The SAP_NEW profile grants unrestricted access to all existing functions for which additional authorization checks have been introduced. Users can therefore continue to work uninterrupted with functions which are subject to new authorization checks which were not previously executed.

Step 8)
1. Press **save**
2. Then the **back button(F3)** button

User will be created!

How to Lock/Unlock a User in SAP

Locking a user

Purpose of locking user is to temporarily deactivate the users so that they cannot longer access the system. Users can be locked in 2 ways:

- Automatically
- Explicitly/Forcefully

Automatically: There are two possibilities when users get lock automatically

- Maximum number of failed attempts: - controlled via the parameter **login/fails_to_user_lock**. If value is set to 3 it means after 3 failed attempts user will be locked.
- Auto unlock time:- "**login/failed_user_auto_unlock**" defines whether user locked due to unsuccessful logon attempts should be automatically removed at midnight.

Explicitly/Forcefully: We can lock and unlock users in 2 ways-
1. Lock single user (**SU01**)
2. Lock multiple user (**SU10**)

Procedure to lock a single user

Step 1) Execute T-code **SU01**

Step 2) Enter username in **User** field.

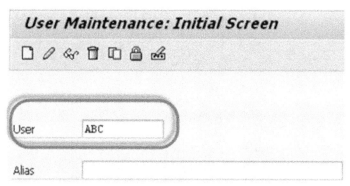

Step 3) Press **Lock/Unlock** button

Step 4) In the next screen, Press **Lock** button again to lock the user.

Procedure to lock multiple users

Step 1) Execute T-code **SU10**

SU10

SAP Easy Access - User Mer

Step 2) Enter users' username in **User** field.

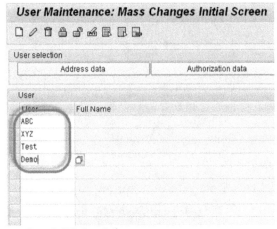

Step 3) Press **Lock/Unlock** button

All the users listed will be locked

Procedure to unlock a user

Step 1) Execute T-code **su01**

Step 2) Enter username in **User** field.

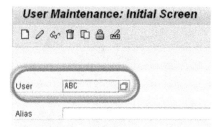

Step 3) Press **Lock/Unlock** button

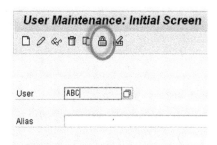

Step 4) Press **Unlock** button

Procedure to unlock multiple users

Step 1) Execute T-code **SU10**

Step 2) Enter users' username in **User** field.

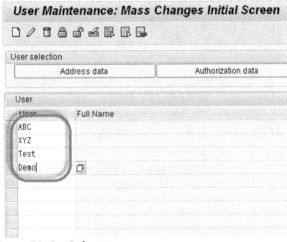

Step 3) Press **Unlock** button

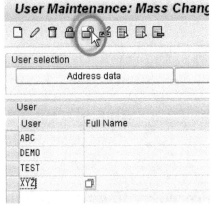

Users will be unlocked

How to Limit Logon Attempts in SAP

Before we learn to limit logon attempts we need to know parameter

What is a parameter?

Parameter is the set of keys and values to manage the SAP system. There are two types of parameters:

1. **Static:** It needs restart. It doesn't effect to the system immediately once you set the value for it.
2. **Dynamic:** It does not need restart. It effects to the system immediately once you set the value for it.

How to view a parameter?

Step 1) Execute T-code RZ11.

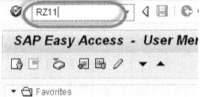

Step 2)
1. Put parameter name *"login/fails_to_session_end"* in text-field. You can put any Parameter name.
2. Click Display

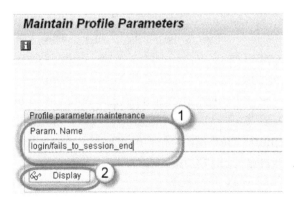

Step 3) The screen below shows the current value set for the parameter by the admin

Display Profile Parameter Attributes

🗋 Documentation

Parameter Name
login/fails_to_session_end

Short Description (Engl.)	Number of invalid login attempts until session end	
Application Area	Logon	🗋
Parameter Type	Integer value	🗋
Changes allowed	Change permitted	🗋
Valid for Operating Sys.	All operating systems	🗋
Minimum	1	
Maximum	99	
Dynam. switchable	☐	
Same on all servers	☐	
Default Value	3	
Profile Value	3	
Current Value	3	

To change a parameter, click the pencil icon and make desired changes

Important Parameters to limit login attempts

- *login/fails_to_session_end*: This parameter specifies the number of times that a user can enter an incorrect password before the system ends the logon attempt. The parameter is to be set to a value lower than the value of parameter
- login/fails_to_user_lock. After N number of failed password attempts system will automatically ends the session. Default value is 3. You can set it to any value between 1 and 99 inclusive.
- *login/fails_to_user_lock*: This parameter specifies the number of times that a user can enter an incorrect password before the system locks the user against further logon attempts. Default value is 12. You can set it to any value between 1 and 99 inclusive.

How to set Password Restrictions in SAP

You can use the following system profile parameters to specify the minimum length of a password and the frequency with which users must change their password.

- *login/min_password_lng*: minimum password length.

    Default value: Three characters. You can set it to any value between 3 and 8.

- *login/password_expiration_time*: number of days after which a password expires

    To allow users to keep their passwords without limit, leave the value set to the default 0.

Specifying Impermissible Passwords

You can prevent users from choosing passwords that you do not want to allow. To prohibit the use of a password, enter it in table USR40. You can maintain table USR40 with Transaction SM30. In USR40, you can specify impermissible passwords generically if you want. There are two wildcard characters:

1. ? stands for a single character
2. stands for a sequence of any combination characters of any length.

123* in table USR40 prohibits any password that begins with the sequence "123."

123 prohibits any password that contains the sequence "123."

AB? prohibits all passwords that begin with "AB" and have one additional character: "ABA", "ABB", "ABC" and so on.

To set restriction for password follow the below procedure:

Step 1) Execute T-code SM30.

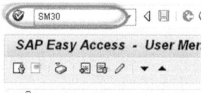

Step 2) Enter the table name USR40 in "Table/View" field.

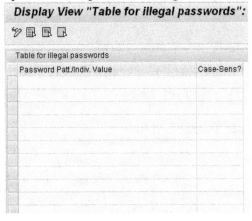

Maintain Table Views: Initial Screen

[H] Find Maintenance Dialog

Table/View   USR40

Restrict Data Range
- ⦿ No Restrictions
- ○ Enter conditions
- ○ Variant

    🖋 Display   ✎ Maintain   🚚 Transport

Step 3) Click Display button.

Table/View   USR40

Restrict Data Range
- ⦿ No Restrictions
- ○ Enter conditions
- ○ Variant

    🖋 Display   ✎ Maintain   🚚

Display

Step 4) Enter password expression string.

Display View "Table for illegal passwords":

🖊 📑 📑 📑

Table for illegal passwords	
Password Patt./Indiv. Value	Case-Sens?

That's it to password management!

Chapter 5. Background Jobs

Background Job Processing

What is a background Job?

Unlike Foreground jobs, Background jobs are non-interactive processes that run behind the normal interactive operations. They run in parallel and do not disturb interactive (foreground) processes and operations.

It is scheduled from SM36. You can analyze it from SM37 by viewing its job log.

Advantages of Background Jobs

- It reduces manual effort & automates the task.
- It can be scheduled as per user's choice.
- It reduces user interaction and can run seamlessly in the background without user input
- Once you define the variant for background job, the user doesn't have to worry about value input in the field. Thus, user confusion is also reduced.
- Ideal for time- consuming/ resource intensive programs which can be scheduled to run in the night (when system load is low).

Background jobs are classified in three categories:

1. **Class A (High/critical Priority):** Some tasks are urgent or critical and must be scheduled with class A priority job. Class A priority reserves one or more background work processes. Users should decide how many background work processes should be assigned to Class A priority job. Suppose a user chooses 2 background work processes for this category then available background work processes for class B and C = (Total number of work processes set in operation modes RZ03)- (Background work processes allowed to class A category).

2. **Class B (Medium Priority)**: Once Class A jobs are completed; Class B job will start executing in the background before class C jobs.
3. **Class C (Low Priority)**: It runs after both class A and class B jobs are completed.

Possible status of background jobs

1. **Scheduled:** You have defined the program name and variant but not defined start condition like Start Date, End Date, and Frequency etc. That means you have not defined when job should be scheduled in system.
2. **Released:** All required criteria are fulfilled for job definition. Start condition is must for the job to be in release status.
3. **Ready:** All the required conditions are met to run the job in a background work process. But job scheduler has put the job in the queue because it is waiting for background work process to be free.
4. **Active:** Job has started running in the background. We cannot change the status of the job once it is in Active status.
5. **Finished:** Job is executed successfully. It means desired task is competed without any error.
6. **Cancelled:** There are two possibilities for this. Administrator has forcefully cancelled the job or there might be some issue with job. You can investigate this from Job logs.

How to schedule the background job?

You can schedule the background job using SM36. Planned or immediate jobs can be scheduled.
Step 1) Execute T-code **SM36**.

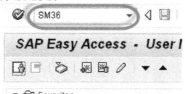

Step 2) Fill the job name, priority (**A/B/C**) and the target server. Background jobs once scheduled on a target server run on that server. Main purpose of defining target server is the workload balancing.

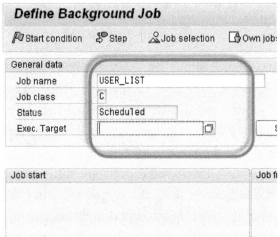

Step 3) Click on "**spool list recipient**". You will get output in your mailbox. You can check email from **SBWP**.

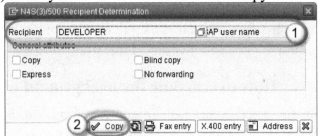

Step 4) Insert your **SAP** username and click copy button.

Step 5) Click **Step** button to define ABAP program, variant's details, etc.

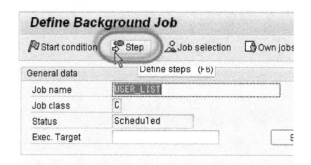

Step 6) Define program name, variant details.

1. Enter your program name, Variant name in the field. If you have not created variant as per your requirement, then leave it blank.
2. Press save button.

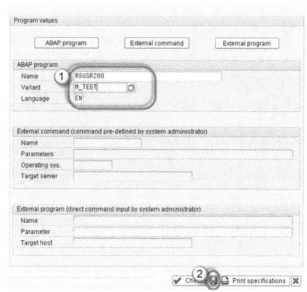

Step 7) Once you schedule the job you will get the following screen.

Step List Overview

🖉 🗋 🖎 🖧 🖑 🗑 🖳 Spool   ⊞ ◀ ◀ ▶ ▶

No.	Program name/command	Prog. type	Spool list	Parameters	User	Lang.
1	RSUSR200	ABAP		M_TEST	DEVELOPER	EN

Step 8) Click Start conditions to fill start date, end date, frequency, etc. for job. If you do not specify start condition, **then job will always remain in scheduled status.** A job in scheduled status will never run.

1. Click on **Date/Time (For periodic jobs).** If you click "Immediate" then job will start running right away. But it will not be set as periodic job. It is like "**press and run**".

2. Define job's start date/time, end date/time. The job will be released only once it meets its **Scheduled start date/time.**

3. Press periodic values.

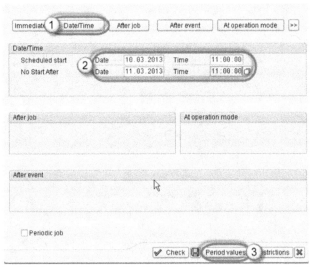

Step 9) Click on Hourly/Daily/Weekly period to define the frequency of the job as per your requirement. We will select Another Period

Step 10) Here you specify the recurring criteria of the job. For example, you can have the Job run after every 5 days from the Start Date. Here we select job to run every 10 minutes

Step 11) Click on **save** button.

Step 12) Click on **save** again.

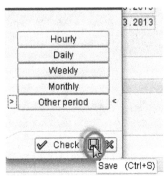

Step 13) Click **save** again

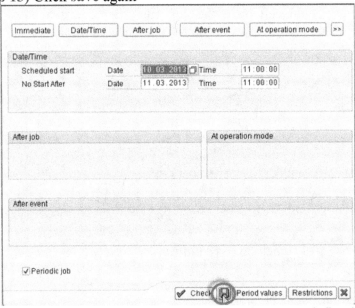

Step 14) Once **Job step and start conditions** are defined the following window will appear.

Step 15) Press **save.**

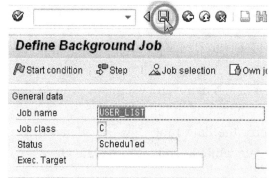

Step 16) Go to **SM37** to know the status of the job.

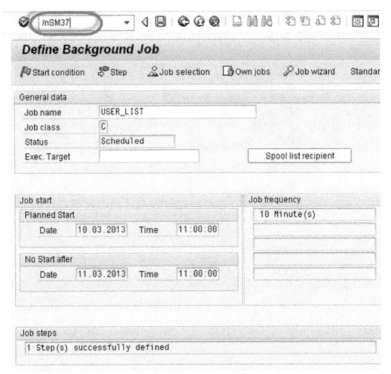

Step 17) Select your criteria for the job which you want to monitor.

1. Put your job name and username who scheduled the job.
2. Select the status of the job.
3. Specify the date range. In our scenario, we just specify the end date while keeping From Date Open.

Simple Job Selection

⊕ Execute   ⊠ Extended job selection   ▣ Information

		①
Job name	USER_LIST	
User name	DEVELOPER	

Job status   ②

☐ Planned   ☑ Released   ☑ Ready   ☐ Active   ☐ Finished   ☐ Canceled

Job start condition

From 🗓   To 🗓 13.03.2013 ③
From 🕐   To 🕐

or after event: ▼

Step 18) You will get the following screen. Look at the status, it's a released means start conditions are met, and the job is in the queue is waiting for **background work process to be free.**

```
Selected        job names:  USER_LIST
Selected user names:        DEVELOPER
```

☐ Scheduled   ☑ Released   ☑ Ready   ☐ Active   ☐ Finished   ☐ Canceled
☐ Event controlled   Event ID:
☐ ABAP program   Program name :

Job	Spool	Job Doc	Job CreatedB	Status	S
☐ USER_LIST			DEVELOPER	Released	
*Summary					

How to Reschedule a background job

Rescheduled jobs will not run in the future. Remember, you cannot reschedule the job once it's in **active** status.

Step 1) Execute **SM37.**

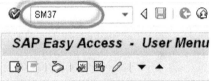

Step 2) Fill the criteria.

1. Job name and username by which job is scheduled.
2. Select the status. To reschedule the job, you can only select Released/Ready status.
3. Specify the date range.
4. Press Execute(F8) button.

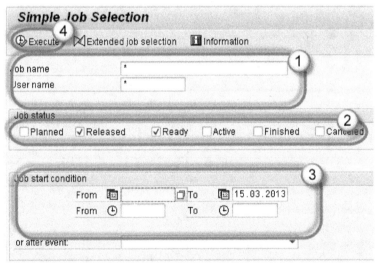

Step 3) Select specified job and press **Job -> (Released -> Scheduled).**

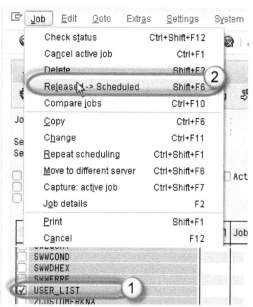

Step 4) You will find the message in the status bar once you press **"Released -> Scheduled"**.

How to Monitor a Background Job in SAP

Monitoring background job is important because once you schedule the job it might be cancelled due to some error. To investigate the root cause use SM37.

Step 1) Execute T-code **SM37**.

Step 2) Fill the required criteria.

1. **Job name and username** (who scheduled the job). You can put * to get details of all jobs scheduled by all the users.
2. Select job status which you want to monitor. If you find that a background job is not completed, select Cancelled status.
3. Put the date range as per your requirement.

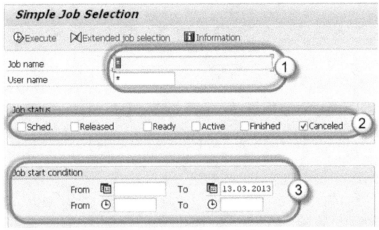

Step 3) You will get a screen as shown below.

Step 4) Click on **Job Log** button to trace the error due to which job was cancelled.

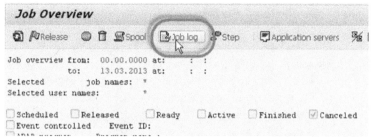

Step 5) You will get the following details. In the below example, job was cancelled since there was an issue with RFC connection to the remote system. As a resolution use SM59 to check if there is an authorization issue to the remote system.

Date	Time	Message text
07.03.2013	19:00:24	RFC connection check failed. Check connection
07.03.2013	19:00:24	Job cancelled after system exception ERROR_MESSAGE

Sometimes jobs in Active status may also cause an issue.

You may face issues like tablespaces are full, duplicate job is running with the same name and timing, job is selecting or updating large data, etc.

You can also check such jobs from SM37. Follow the procedure as below.

Step 1) Execute **SM37**.

Step 2) Fill the required criteria.

1. Job name and username (by which job is scheduled).
2. Select job status which you want to monitor. **If you find a system performance issue or if a task is not completed for a very long time, then select active status.**
3. Put the date range as per your requirement.

Simple Job Selection

⊕ Execute   ☒ Extended job selection   🛈 Information

Job name	**1** *
User name	*

Job status

2 ☐ Sched. ☐ Released ☐ Ready ☑ Active ☐ Finished ☐ Cancelec

Job start condition

3 From 🔢 [   ] ☐ To 🔢 13.03.2013
From 🕐 [   ]   To 🕐 [   ]

Step 3) Consider **Duration** column (which signifies the job is running since n seconds). If you find a large number in duration, then investigate the job details from job log. Some jobs use a large number of data. Using SE16 check table entries for the tables used by   the   job.

Status	Start date	Start time	Duration(sec.)
Active	13.03.2013	16:02:06	4.796
			4.796

Sometimes jobs show to be in Active Status even though they are completed.

How to correct them? Follow the below set of procedure:

Step 1) As shown above, Execute T-code **SM37** and select the job with active status.

Step 2) Select the **active** job which is causing problem.

Job		Ln	Job CreatedB
☑ BI WRITE PROT TO APPLLOG			DDIC

Step 3) Click the **Job->Check status**.

Job **1** t Goto Extras Settings System	
Check status	Ctrl+Shift-l **2**
Cancel active job	Ctrl+F1
Delete	Shift+F2
Released -> Scheduled	Shift+F6
Compare jobs	Ctrl+F10

Step 4) In the status bar of the window you will find as below message. **This will repair Job Status if there was a problem**

☑ 1 jobs were checked and 0 jobs were corrected

Step 5) If still job is in running status then go to **SM50**. Below screen will open. Have a look in "**Reasn**" column which shows any errors or exceptional issue. Investigate it further.

Process Overview

No	Ty.	PID	Status	Reasn	Start	Err	Sem	CPU
0	DIA	13092	running		Yes	I		
1	DIA	28798	waiting		Yes			
2	DIA	1824	running		Yes			
3	DIA	19616	waiting		Yes			
4	DIA	19672	waiting		Yes			
5	DIA	28014	waiting		Yes			
6	UPD	16721	waiting		Yes			
7	ENQ	18915	waiting		Yes			
8	BGD	6535	waiting		Yes			
9	BGD	24024	running		Yes			
10	SPO	23530	waiting		Yes			
11	UP2	21179	waiting		Yes			

How to Delete a Background Job

Why Delete Background Job?

Old jobs occupy space on the system. To avoid any inconsistencies within the system normally we delete the logs. Because if the file system gets full your SAP system will crash!

You can delete jobs in two ways:

1. Multiple jobs at once.
2. Single job deletion.

Delete Multiple Jobs at once

The best way to do this is use report **RSBTCDEL2 (New version of RSBTCDEL)**. Old job logs will be deleted and will not show in the job overview.

Step 1) Execute T-code **SE38**.

Step 2) Put the program name in the field as **RSBRCDEL2**.

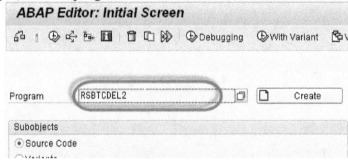

Step 3) Fill the proper details.

1. Which job do you want to delete? If you put * means all jobs. If you want to delete jobs from a specific user, give Username.

2. Specify Status of Job to be deleted. Specify period of Deletion. For instance, delete jobs older than 14 days. NOTE:

Once the job is in active status, it is impossible to delete them.

3. Specify Commit. Commit value is proportional to program performance. **If the commit value is high, then job deletion will run faster.** Recommended value is >= 1000.
4. Check Test run to simulate the deletion. Jobs will not be deleted. Once you are sure only then uncheck the **Test run**.
5. Press Execute.

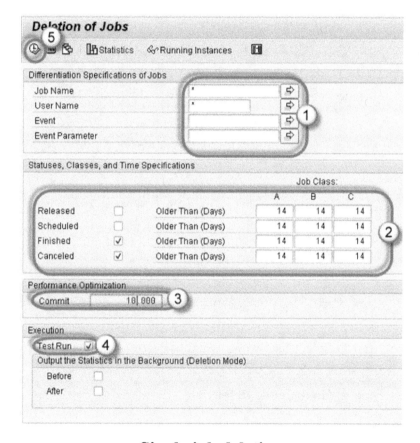

Single job deletion

You can also delete a single job from **SM37**.
Step 1) Execute **SM37**.

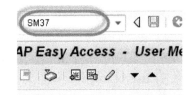

Step 2) Fill your **criteria**.

1. Job name and username
2. Status of the job.
3. Select the date range.

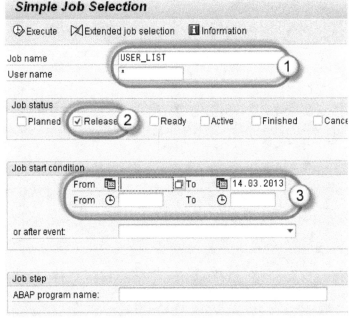

Step 3) Select the job you want to delete

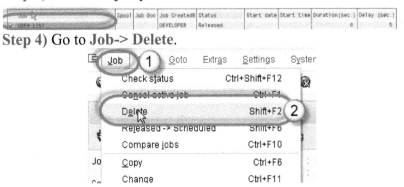

Step 4) Go to **Job-> Delete**.

You can also delete the jobs from OS level under directory
**/usr/sap/<SID>/SYS/global/<CLNT>JOBLG.
Folder.**

But deletion from OS level may cause **Times** inconsistency issue. To remove inconsistencies, go to **SP12-> Consistency check**. Once you get the list, delete the objects.

Normally, Job- **SAP_REORG_JOBS** (Program to Delete old background jobs) must be scheduled within the system with program **RSBTCDEL2** at daily frequency.

Chapter 6. Transport Management System

Introduction to Transport Management System (TMS)

Why do we need a Transport System?

Development System   Quality-Assurance System   Production System

The CTS components play an important role in the overall development and customization environment.

CTS is an instrument for:
- Administering & controlling new development requests.
- Managing transports
- Recording of where and by whom changes are made
- Configuring systems landscape

Overview of CTS Components

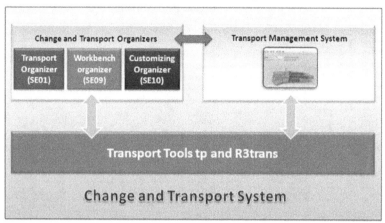

- **CTO (Change and Transport Organizer)** – It's the main tool for managing, browsing, and registering the changes done on the repository and customizing objects. It's the central point for organizing the development projects. SE01 is the transaction with new extended view.

- **(TMS) Transport Management System** – Is used to move, manage, control, copy development objects and customizing settings in an orderly fashion across SAP systems in a landscape through pre-defined transport routes (RFC Connections). The transport process basically consists of exporting of objects out of the source SAP system and importing them into the target SAP system/s.

- **Transport Tools** – The actual transports happen in the back-end at the OS level using transport tools, which are part of SAP Kernel and includes the program *R3trans* and the transport control program *tp*.

SAP System-Landscape

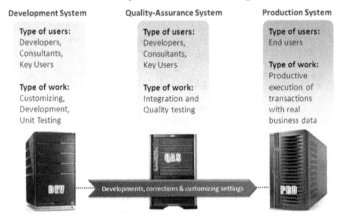

The system landscape (also known as *SAP System Group*) is the arrangement of SAP servers. Ideally, in an SAP environment, a three-system landscape is recommended. It consists of the:

1. Development Server – DEV
2. Quality Assurance Server - QAS
3. Production Server - PRD.

Transport cycle in a very basic sense, is the release of new Developments/ Customizing Changes from DEV which are imported in both Quality and Production systems. However, import in PRD can happen only once integration testing and quality check has been performed in QAS (and marked as checked).

What is Customizing? How does TMS help in Customizing

- Customizing is a process to adapt the SAP system according to the customer's need. To perform the customizing, users and consultants take help of SAP Reference Implementation Guide (IMG), which is accessible through transaction SPRO.

- Customizing is ideally done in DEV. The Transport Organizer (SE01) is used in conjunction with IMG to record and transport customized changes further.

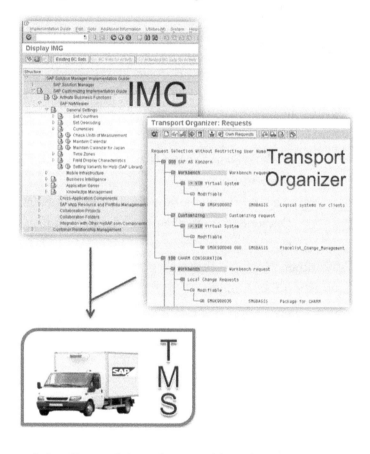

Most of the Customizing changes (though, not all) are client-specific, i.e., the changes are supposed to be reflected in a client only and not intended for all the system clients. When the Transport

Request is exported, it extracts the relevant table entries from the database of the SAP system and copies them to the transport directory. Relevant table entries are locked when the customizing transaction is being used. However, they are unlocked as soon as the changes are saved to a Transport Request.

Repository and Development Changes

- Apart from customizing already existing objects, new developments are also required in most of the cases. Development object is any object that is created (developed) by you in SAP system.
- Collection of all such objects (client-specific or cross-client) is called **Repository**.
- Development is mostly done with the help of ABAP Workbench (SE80); therefore, such changes are also known as Workbench Changes.
- Examples:
    o ABAP Dictionary Objects: Tables, Domains, Data elements, etc.
    o ABAP Programs, function modules, menus, screens
    o Documents, Application defined transport-objects, etc.
- Workbench is also fully integrated with TMS, to record and transport the changes.

Most of the Workbench changes (though, not all), are **cross-client**, i.e. changes will be reflected in all the system clients of the target system. Objects transported from the source system overwrite objects in the target system that has the same names.

Clients and the type of Data in SAP System

- Conceptually, client is a technical and organizational independent unit, that contains its own set of data (Master Data, Application/ Operational data, Customizing Data)
- Clients create separate environments for users from different user groups or with a different purpose, within same SAP system, without using different database.
- From Technical point of view, client is specified using 3-digit numeric ID, which also acts as the value for the table field 'MANDT', in case of client-specific jobs.

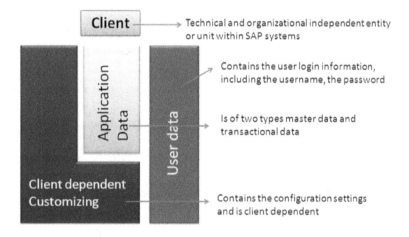

Among client specific data, there are 3 types of data:

- **User Master Data** contains the user login information, including the username, the password and the user defaults, the authorization profiles or roles, and the other useful information such as user groups, communication and so on. This data is physically present in a specific set of tables (the USR* tables).
- **Customizing Data** contains the configuration settings to customize organizational structure and the business processes for the companies implementing SAP. This data is client

dependent and is stored in tables known as customizing tables.

- **Application Data** are also client dependent and normally users distinguish two types' master data and transactional data.

    1. Master Data such as vendor master, material master (tables such as MARA)
    2. Transactional data such as sales order, financial documents, Production Orders (POs) and so on.

Client Customization Options

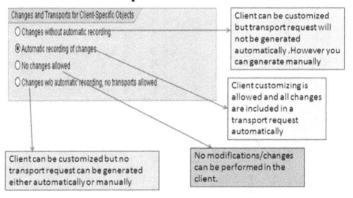

Transport Directory and Its configuration

SAP Transport Directory:

- It is the global transport directory (/usr/sap/trans), which is a shared location (residing in the Domain Controller System) among all the member systems of a landscape (system group). It also contains certain subdirectories, that are created automatically during the installation of the SAP system. This is mandatory for setting up the Transport Management System.

- Basically, Transport Directory is the location where all the changes are saved (in the form of files) after they are released from DEV. Therefore, it acts as a source for the changes to be eventually imported in DEV and PRD. Hence, we should ensure that the transport directory is shared properly among all the systems in a landscape.

As an example, in Windows NT, the shared directory location can be accessed using the following address: \\<SAPTRANSHOST>\sapmnt\trans where SAPTRANSHOST (Domain Controller System's address) is defined in hosts file in Windows Directory of all SAP systems in the landscape. Domain Controller – is one of the systems in a landscape that act as an overall controller for change management and transport process in the landscape. Domain Controller is chosen (out of D / Q / P) by the team of system administrators, based on system availability and the time of installation.

Main Subdirectories:

- **Cofiles:** Contains Change Request Information files with complete details and commands.
- **Data Files:** Contains the actual values and data to be used in implementing the change.
- **Log:** Contains Transport logs, traces or statistics, used for trouble-shooting, in case any error occurs in the transport process.
- **EPS:** Download directory for advanced corrections and support packages

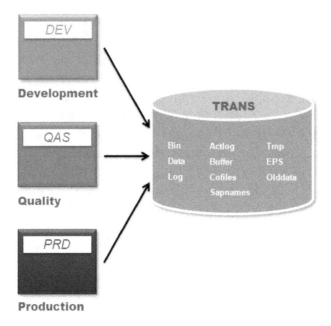

Other Subdirectories are:

- **bin:** Configuration files for tp (Transport Program) and TMS
- **olddata:** Old Exported Data for archival or deletion
- **actlog:** Action logs for all requests and tasks
- **buffer:** Transport buffer for each system declaring the transports to be imported
- **sapnames:** Information regarding transport requests made by respective users
- **tmp:** Temporary and data log files

Setting up of Transport Directory and TPPARAM

- While configuring TMS, one of the main pre-requisite is to setting up the Transport Directory and the Transport Parameter file.
- It ensures that the Directory is shared properly among all the systems in a Landscape, for that all the systems taking part in the group/landscape are to be included in the global configuration file TPPARAM (transport parameter file),

located under the bin subdirectory of /use/sap/trans. We should ensure that the entries for all the participating systems are made in this file.

- In case, any entry is missing, copy another system's entry and change the values (for instance, System ID, Host name)
- At the time of installation, transport directory & the sub-directories are created automatically, including an initially configured template of TPPARAM file.

Operating System Tools - TP and R3trans

TP – The Transport Control Program:
- tp is the SAP program that administrators use for performing and planning transports between systems and also in upgrades of the SAP systems. This is used by the CTO and TMS.
- Actually, tp uses other special tools/programs and utilities to perform its functions. Mainly, it calls R3trans utility program. However, it also offers a more extensive control of the transport process, ensuring the correct sequence of the exported/imported objects, to avoid severe inconsistencies in the system, which may arise due to wrong sequence.
- tp is in the standard runtime directory of the SAP system: /usr/sap/SYS/<SID>/exe/run. It is automatically copied in the installation process.
- As a pre-requisite, the tp global parameter file (TPPARAM), must be maintained, specifying at least, hostnames of the systems taking part in the transport process.
- tp is mainly used for performing imports in target systems. It uses utilities called Import Dispatchers – RDDIMPDP & RDDIMPD_CLIENT_<nnn>, these are ought to be scheduled as background jobs in every system where imports will be performed. If for any reason they are deleted, we can schedule these jobs by running report RDDNEWPP.

- These jobs are *"event triggered"*, meaning that **tp** sends a signal (an event) to the R/3 system and the job starts. These events are named as **SAP_TRIGGER_RDDIMPDP** and **SAP_TRIGGER_RRDIMPDP_CLIENT**.

R3trans – The Transport Control Program:
- **R3trans** is the SAP system transport program that can be used for transporting data between different SAP systems. It is normally not used directly, but called from the **tp** control program or by the SAP upgrade utilities.
- **tp** controls the transports and generates the r3trans control files, but does not connect to the database itself. All the "real work" is done from **R3trans**.
- It supports the transporting of data between systems running on different OS and even different DB.

How to configure TMS (Transport Management System)

TMS Configuration

- TMS is the transport tool that assists the CTO for central management of all transport functions. TMS is used for performing:
  - o Defining Transport Domain Controller.
  - o Configuring the SAP system Landscape
  - o Defining the Transport Routes among systems within the system Landscape
  - o Distributing the configuration
- **Transport Domain Controller** – one of the systems from the landscape that contains complete configuration information and controls the system landscape whose transports are being maintained jointly. For availability and

security reasons, this system is normally the Productive system.

Within transport domain all systems must have a unique System Ids and only one of these systems is identified as the domain controller, the transport domain controller is the system where all TMS configuration settings are maintained. Any changes in to the configuration settings are distributed to all systems in the landscape. A transport group is one or more systems that share a common transport directory. Transport Domain – comprises all the systems and the transport routes in the landscape. Landscape, Group and Domain are the terms that are used synonymously by system administrators.

Step 1) Setting up the Domain Controller
- Log on to the SAP system, which is decided to be the Domain Controller, in client **000** and enter the transaction code **STMS.**
- If there is no Domain Controller already, system will prompt you to create one. When the Transport Domain is created for the first time, following activities happen in the background:
  - o Initiation of the Transport Domain / Landscape / Group
  - o Creating the user **TMSADM**
  - o Generating the RFC Destinations required for R/3 Configurations, TMSADM is used as the target login user.
  - o Creating **DOMAIN.CFG** file
    in usr/sap/trans/**bin** directory – This file contains the TMS configuration and is used by systems and domains for checking existing configurations.

Step 2) Transaction STMS

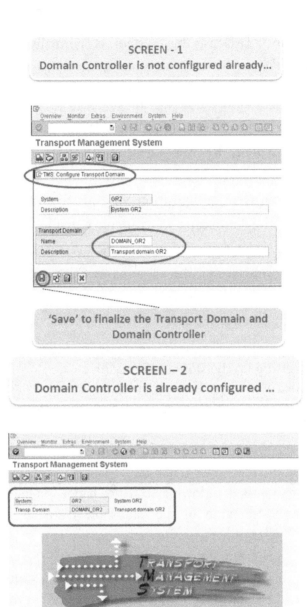

Transport Management System

TMS: Configure Transport Domain

| System | GR2 |
| Description | System GR2 |

Transport Domain
| Name | DOMAIN_GR2 |
| Description | Transport domain GR2 |

'Save' to finalize the Transport Domain and Domain Controller

Transport Management System

| System | GR2 | System GR2 |
| Transp. Domain | DOMAIN_GR2 | Transport domain GR2 |

You are logged onto the domain controller

Step 3) Adding SAP systems to the Transport Domain
- Log on to SAP systems (to be added in the domain) in client 000 and start transaction STMS.

- TMS will check the configuration file DOMAIN.CFG and will automatically propose to join the domain (if the domain controller already created). 'Select' the proposal and save your entries.
- For security purpose, system status will still be in 'waiting' status, to be included in the transport domain.
- For complete acceptance, login to Domain Controller System (Client 000) -> **STMS** -> **Overview** -> **Systems**. New system will be visible there. From the menu choose **'SAP System'** -> **Approve**.

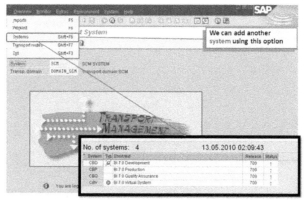

Step 4) Configuring Transport Routes
- **Transport Routes** – are the different routes created by system administrators and are used to transmit changes between the systems in a system group/landscape. There are two types of transport routes:
  - **Consolidation** (From DEV to QAS) – Transport Layers are used
  - **Delivery** (From QAS to PRD) – Transport Layers not required
- **Transport Layer** – is used to group the changes of similar kinds, for example, changes are done in development objects of same class/category/package, logically should be sent through same transport route. Therefore, transport layers are assigned to all objects coming from DEV system. Layers are

used in Consolidation routes, however after testing happens in QAS, layers are not used and the changes are moved using single routes towards PRD system.

Package – (formerly known as Development Class) is a way to classify the objects logically belonging to the same category or project. A package can also be an object itself and is assigned with a specific transport layer (in consolidation route), therefore, changes made in any of the development object belonging to a Package, will be transmitted towards target system through a designated Transport Layer only, or else the change will be saved as a Local (non-transportable) modification.

How to configure Transport Routes and Layers

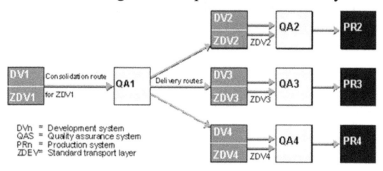

Consolidation routes – We need to establish a consolidation route for each transport layer. Development/ Integration system is taken as the source of these consolidation routes. Quality assurance/ Consolidation system as the transport target. Any modified objects that have a consolidation route for their transport layer can be included in change/transport requests. After the request has been released, the objects can be imported into the consolidation system. If the changes are made to the objects with no consolidation route set-up (or in Customizing requests without a transport target) for their transport layer, such changes will be automatically taken as local change requests, i.e., not-transportable. Only one consolidation route per transport layer per system can be set-up.

Setting up Transport Routes

Once the Domain and other systems of a landscape are defined, we need to connect them with the help of proper transport routes (and layers). As for many customers' systems landscape fall into the same categories, the TMS provides some standard system groups that can be used for easily defining routes. When standard options are used, routes are generated automatically; we can select one of the following options:

- Single System
- Two-System landscape: DEV and PRD
- Three System landscape: DEV, QAS and PRD

If we need to define a more complex transport system, we can also use standard options initially and thereafter define additional consolidation and delivery routes.

Transport Routes – Standard Configuration

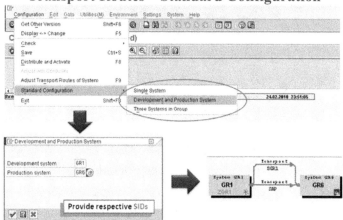

Transport Routes – Manual Configuration

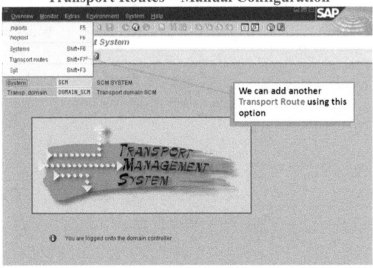

We can add another Transport Route using this option

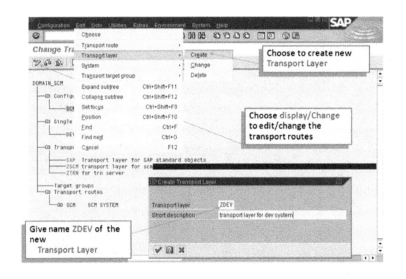

Choose to create new Transport Layer

Choose display/Change to edit/change the transport routes

Give name ZDEV of the new Transport Layer

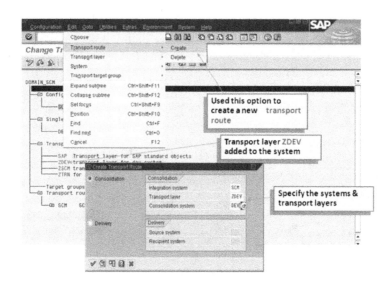

Used this option to create a new transport route

Transport layer ZDEV added to the system

Specify the systems & transport layers

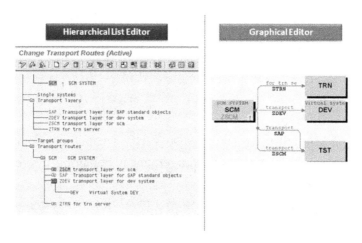

Hierarchical List Editor

Graphical Editor

Change Transport Routes (Active)

Transport Routes

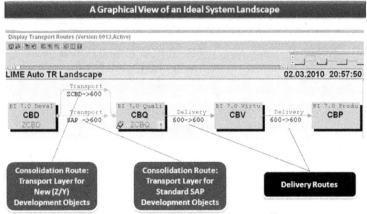

Distributing and Verifying the Configuration

- After the transport route settings are made or modified in domain controller, all other member systems of the domain ought to know the new configuration. For that we need to execute **STMS -> Transport Routes Screen -> Systems Overview -> Configuration -> Distribution and Activate Configuration**

- Additionally, we should also verify various check-points, to ensure that the whole arrangement is behaving in the desired manner:
  - o For **RFC Connections:** Overview -> Systems -> SAP System ->Check -> Connection Test
  - o For **Network**: Transport Routes Overview -> Config. -> Check -> Request Consistency
  - o For *tp* & **TPPARAM**: System Overview Screen -> SAP System -> Check -> Transport Tool

What is Transport Request? How to Import/Export it & check logs?

What is a Transport Request?

- **Transport Requests (TRs)** – are also known as Change Requests. It is a kind of 'Container / Collection' of changes that are made in the development system. It also records the information regarding the type of change, purpose of transport, request category and the target system.
- Each TR contains one or more change jobs, also known as change **Tasks** (minimum unit of transportable change). Tasks are stored inside a TR, just like multiple files are stored in some folder. TR can be released only once all the tasks inside a TR are completed, released or deleted.
- Change Task is a list of objects that are modified by a user. Each task can be assigned to (and released by) only one user, however multiple users can be assigned to each Transport Request (as it can contain multiple tasks). Tasks are not transportable by themselves, but only as a part of TR.

Change requests are named in a standard format as: **<SID>K<Number>** [*Not modifiable by system administrators*]
- **SID** – System ID
- **K** – Is fixed keyword/alphabet
- **Number** – can be anything from a range starting with 900001

Example: **DEVK900030**

Tasks also use the same naming convention, with 'numbers' consecutive to the number used in TR containing them.
For Example, Tasks in the above-mentioned TR Example can be named as: **DEVK900031, DEVK900032 ...**

- The project manager or designated lead is responsible to create a TR and assign the project members to the TR by creating task/s for each project member.
- Hence, she/he is the owner with control of all the changes that are recorded in that TR and therefore, she/he can only release that TR.
- However, assigned project members can release their respective change tasks, once completed.

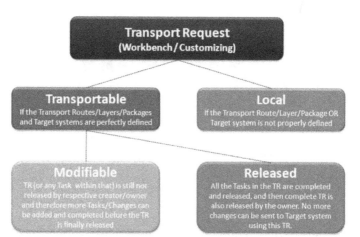

Workbench Request – contains repository objects and *'cross-client'* customizing objects. These requests are responsible for making changes in the ABAP workbench objects.

Customizing Request – contains objects that belong to *'client-specific'* customizing. As per client settings these requests are automatically recorded as per when users perform customizing settings and a target system is automatically assigned as per the transport layer (if defined).

SE01 – Transport Organizer – Extended View

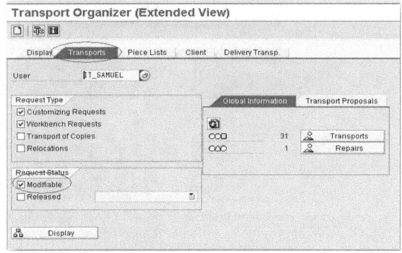

Create a Change Request

- Change Request can be created in two ways:
  - **Automatic** – Whenever creating or modifying an object, or when performing customizing settings, system itself displays the 'Dialog box' for creating a change request or mention name of an already created request, if available.
  - **Manually** – Create the change request from the Transport Organizer, and then enter required attributes and insert objects.

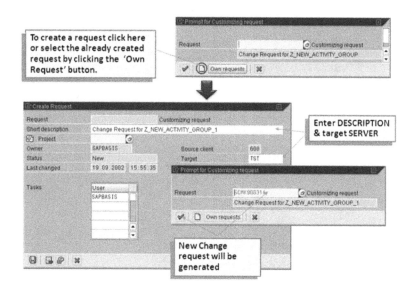

To create a request click here or select the already created request by clicking the 'Own Request' button.

Enter DESCRIPTION & target SERVER

New Change request will be generated

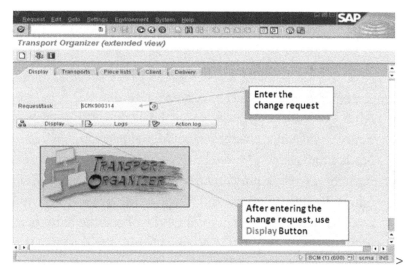

Enter the change request

After entering the change request, use Display Button

Release the Transport Request (Export Process)

- Position the cursor on the TR name or a Task name & choose the Release icon (Truck), a record of the TR is automatically added to the appropriate import queues of the systems defined in the TMS.

- Releasing and importing a request generates export & import logs.

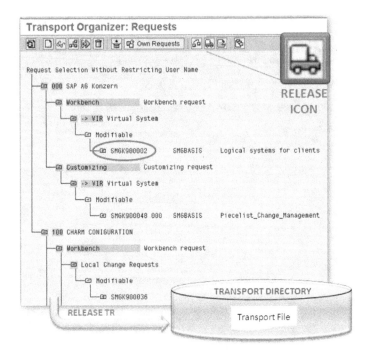

The Import Process

Importing TRs into the target system

- After the request owner releases the Transport Requests from Source system, changes should appear in quality and production system; *however, this is not an automatic process.*

- As soon as the export process completes (releasing of TRs), relevant files (Cofiles and Data files) are created in the common transport directory at OS level and the entry is made in the **Import Buffer** (OS View) / **Import Queue** (SAP App. View) of the QAS and PRD.

- Now to perform the import, we need to access the import queue and for that we need to execute transaction code **STMS** -> **Import Button** OR select **Overview** -> **Imports**

- It will show the list of systems in the current domain, description and number of requests available in Import Queue and the status.

Import Queue -> is the list of TRs available in the common directory and are ready to be imported in the target system, this is the SAP Application View, at the OS level it is also known as **Import Buffer.**

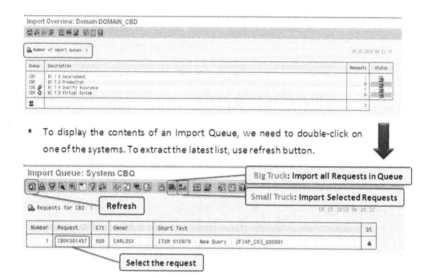

- To display the contents of an Import Queue, we need to double-click on one of the systems. To extract the latest list, use refresh button.

Big Truck: Import all Requests in Queue

Small Truck: Import Selected Requests

Refresh

Select the request

The Import status

Import Queue shows some standard 'status icons' in the last column, here are the icons with their meanings, as defined by SAP:

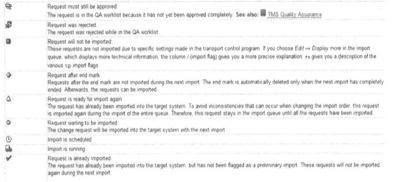

In case, a request is not added automatically in the import queue/buffer, even though the OS level files are present, then we can add such requests by the following method, however, we should know the name of intended TR:

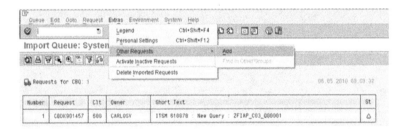

Import History

We can also check the previous imports that happened in the system as follows:

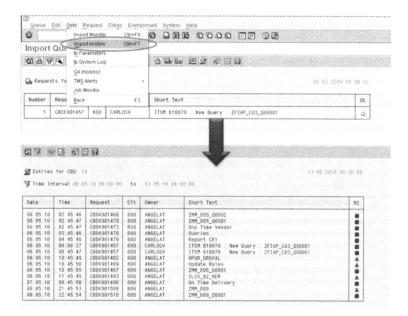

Transport logs and return codes

- After the transport, system administrator must check whether it was performed properly or not, for that SAP has provided us with the following type of logs (**SE01 -> GOTO -> Transport Logs**):
  - **Action Log** – which displays actions that have taken place: exports, test import, import and so forth.
  - **Transport Logs** – which keep a record of the transport log files.
- One of the important information provided by logs are the return codes:
  - **0:** The export was successful.
  - **4:** Warning was issued but all objects were transported successfully.

- o **8:** A warning was issued and at least one object could not be transported successfully.
- o **12 or higher:** A critical error had occurred, generally not caused by the objects in the request.

Chapter 7. Patch Administration

Support Package & Stack Updates – Ultimate Guide

What is a Support Package?

- When an end user of SAP finds a bug in the SAP product, he reports the same to SAP support. SAP programmers inspect the bug and develop a correction for the bug. **This correction is known as SNOTE (SAP Note).**

- With time, multiple end users, report bugs for which SAP releases SNOTE. SAP collects all these corrections in one place and this collection is called SUPPORT PACKAGE. This support package also includes enhancements to earlier versions of SAP.

- In simple words collection of SAP NOTES is called as SUPPORT PACKAGE.

- Support Packages are implemented in SAP system using Transaction SPAM (Support Package Manager)

What is Support Package Stack (SPS)?

The Support Package Stack is a list of ABAP and Java Support Packages for all software components (SC) included in SAP NetWeaver. It is used to bring each Software Component of SAP NetWeaver to a defined Support Pack (SP) level.

Support Package Stack, commonly known as STACK bundles all required components or individual patches that are already tested together and recommended applying as SPS instead of individual patch (until and unless you face some problem which requires certain components to be patched).

Go to *http://service.sap.com/sp-stacks/*, select your NW version to check the current SPS level and other details.

What are Support Pack Stack version numbers?

Support Package Stacks have a release number, and a Stack number, Example, SAP NetWeaver '04 Support Package Stack 11.

Each software component has a separate sequence of Support Packages. The following list contains the technical names of many of components and the notation for their Support Packages:

- COP (Component Package):
- SAP_APPL (SAP APPL Support Package): SAPKH<rel><no>
- SAP_BASIS (Basis Support Package): SAPKB<rel><no>
- SAP_ABAP (Application Basis SP): SAPKA<rel><no>
- SAP_HR (SAP HR Support Package): SAPKE<rel><no>
- SAP_SCM (SCM Support Package): SAPKY<rel><no>
- SAP_BW (BW Support Package): SAPKW<rel><no>
- SAP_CRM (CRM Support Package): SAPKU<rel><no>

Pre-requisites for Support Package implementation:

- Support packages should be always applied in client 000.
- The user to be used for the support package implementation must have authorizations equivalent to DDIC or SAP*
- Call the transaction SPAM and see if any previous Support Package import is incomplete. You can proceed ahead unless the previous support package import is successful.
- Ensure that there is enough space in the transport directory. The transport directory is located at /usr/sap/trans

Steps to Upgrade the Support Package:

Step 1) Download Support Packs

Support Packages are available in SAP Support Portal, under service.sap.com/patches.

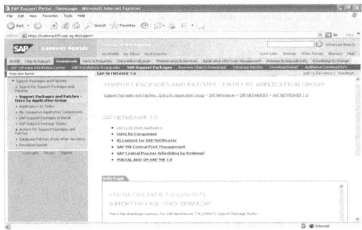

Step 2) Loading Support Packages:

To load support packages, we have two options: -

1. From Application Server
2. From Front End

From Application Server

1. Download the support packages from *service marketplace* and save them at OS level in directory /usr/sap/trans.
2. Uncompress these files using sapcar executable

<code>sapcar -xvf <support package name></code>

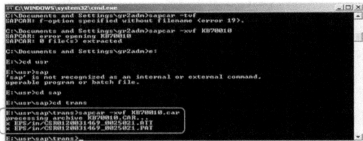

After uncompressing the support packages at OS level the .PAT and. ATT files are stored in /usr/sap/trans/EPS/in directory.

Next, load the Support Packages into SAP system by choosing Support *Package -->Load Package --> From Application Server*

From Front End

Choose Support Package --> Load Packages --> From Front End

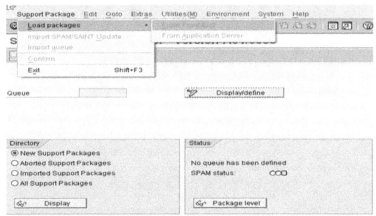

Step 3) SPAM/SAINT Update:

A SPAM/SAINT Update contains updates and improvements to Support Package Manager (SPAM) and Add-On Installation Tool (SAINT). There is always one SPAM update for each release. SPAM/SAINT update is mandatory before any support package upgrade.

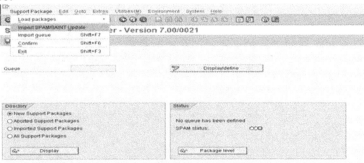

Step 4) Defining Queue

Queue contains the Support Packages available for the different SAP Components installed in your system. This Queue information is derived from the support pack uploaded in Step 2.

1. On the initial screen in Support Package Manager, choose Display/Define.
2. A list of installed software components (for example, SAP_BASIS, SAP_HR, SAP_BW) is displayed.

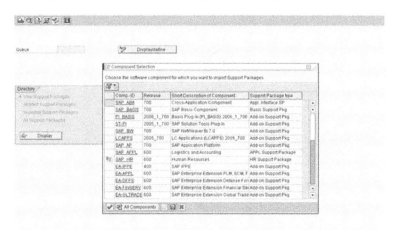

3. Once you select the required component, the current queue appears. This queue contains the Support Packages available for the selected component in your system. If you want to define the queue for another software component, choose *Other Component*. If the displayed queue meets your requirements, you can confirm it by choosing *Confirm Queue*

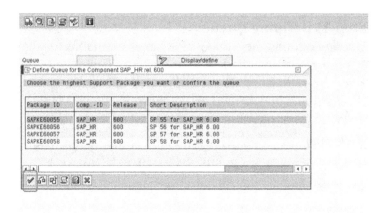

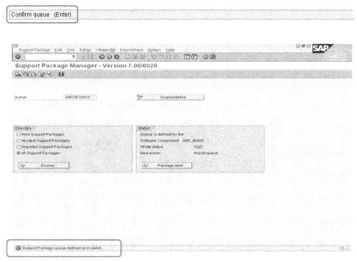

Step 5) Importing Queue.

Once you define a Queue (Step 4) while selecting a particular component (for which we want to upgrade support pack), we need to do 'Import queue' to start importing/applying that selected support pack (as per the standard SAP process).

Choose *Support Package --> Import Queue*

To become familiar with known problems and issues, always read the note mentioned in above screenshot.

The support package import has been started

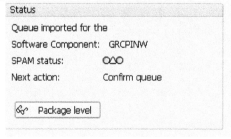

Step 6) Confirming Queue:

Confirm that the queue has been imported successfully into your system. This allows you to import Support Packages in the future. You will not be able to import Support Packages further, if you do not confirm the queue.

Status	
Queue imported for the	
Software Component:	GRCPINW
SPAM status:	⊘⚠○
Next action:	Confirm queue
⚙ Package level	

Once Queue has been imported, SPAM status becomes YELLOW

Confirm successful import of the Support Packages into your system by choosing *Support Package > Confirm.*

Status
No queue has been defined
SPAM status: ○○▢

Checking Logs

- **IMPORT LOG:** It displays logs for *Support Package Manager Phases* that are used by transport control program tp (transport control program).

  Go to-->Import log-->Queue

- **ACTION LOG:** It contains information about *the actions that take place during the individual phases* (while importing the current queue).

It also includes information about the point at which a phase was stopped, as well as detailed error information.

To display the logs for the current queue: Go to-->Action log

- *While the support packages are being imported, logs are made into the tmp directory (path: usr/sap/trans/tmp)*
- *Once the import process is completed logs can be viewed from the log directory (path: usr/sap/trans/log)*

What is SAP Kernel and how to update it?

What is a Kernel?

- The Kernel is the central program which acts as an interface between SAP application and operating system.
- The Kernel consists of the executable programs that reside under the path "/sapmnt/<SID>/exe" (UNIX) or \usr\sap\SID\SYS\exe\run (Windows)
- These files help startup the R/3 system, initialize the memory, create buffers and start managing the requests from users and effectively utilizing of hardware resources.
- The kernel is also responsible for starting and stopping all the application services like dispatcher, message server, collector etc.

Why Kernel Upgrade?

- SAP Kernel is the core of the application. Like all other applications the Kernel contains the executable files (.EXE files for stating various processes in SAP).
- Kernel is the heart of the operating system. It contains those files which are used to run every event in SAP. E.g.|: starting database, shutdowns of database, starting sap, shutdown of sap, saposcol, to uncar the sap files etc.
- That's the reason why when a Kernel upgrade is done it means new versions of the various EXE files replace the older versions.

How to check Kernel Version?

There are many ways to check the Kernel Version:

Method 1) Logon to SAP system and go to SM51 > Release Notes

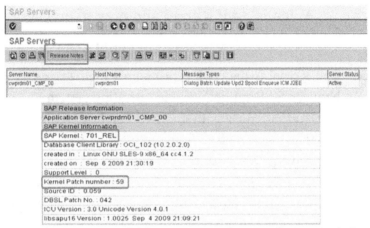

Method 2) Logon to SAP system and go to **System** tab in the menu bar and select **Status**

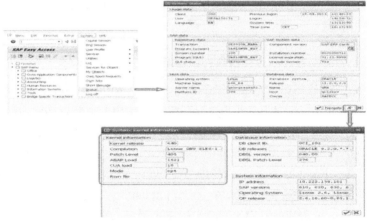

Method 3) Logon in operating system, switch to user <SID>adm and give the command **disp+work**

You can also give **disp+work – version**

```
qriserv:qreadm 5 disp+work

disp+work information
---------------------
kernel release            640

kernel make variant       640_EX2

compiled on               AIX 2 5 00029F1AD300 for "rs6000_64"

compiled for              64 BIT

compilation mode          UNICODE

compile time              Jun  3 2012 20:48:23

update level              0

patch number              405

source id                 0.405


---------------------
supported environment
---------------------
database (SAP, table SVERS)  610
                             620
                             630
                             640
operating system
AIX 2 5
AIX 3 5
AIX 1 6
AIX 1 7
qriserv:qreadm 6>
```

Download Kernel from Service Marketplace

- Go to "SAP Service Marketplace. " (https:\\service.sap.com) You will need your OSS ID and password.
- Then go to Downloads > SAP Support Packages -> Entry by Application Group -> SAP Kernel 6.00 64 Bit -> Select your OS (LINUX/WINDOWS/SOLARIS/AIX) -> Database Dependent and Database Independent Kernel Patch.
- Two SAR files SAPEXE.SAR and SAPEXEDB.SAR are downloaded from Service Marketplace.

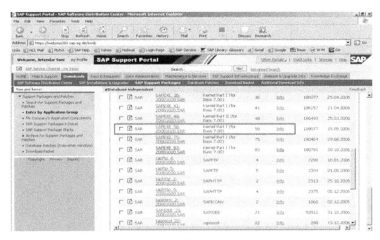

Database Independent

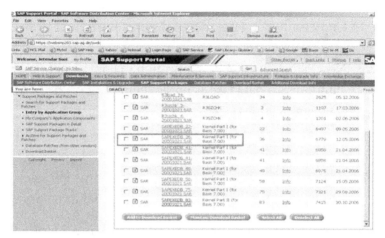

Database Dependent: ORACLE

Kernel Upgrade Steps:

1. Create a new Directory at OS level with enough space. Name of Dir can be "exe_new<ddmmyy>".

2. Transfer these SAPEXEDB.SAR & SAPEXE.SAR files which you have downloaded to the new directory at OS level.

3. Change your current directory to path .SAR files are created (cd /sapmnt/PR2/exe_new20122006). Check the directory path with command 'pwd' to ensure you are in the same dir (exe_new<ddmmyy>).

4. Now uncompress these .SAR files by sapcar exe. The command used for the same would be

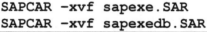

```
SAPCAR -xvf sapexe.SAR
SAPCAR -xvf sapexedb.SAR
```

5. Now create one more directory in that path with the name "exe_old<ddmmyy>". Take the backup of existing kernel.

Copy (only copy not move) the existing kernel from exe directory to "exe_old<ddmmyy>"

6. Now stop the SAP application. (For kernel upgrade the shutdown of database is not essential but we need to stop the SAP application)

```
stopsap r3
```

7. Then copy the files from the new kernel directory exe_new<ddmmyy> to the existing kernel directory exe

```
cp -rp /sapmnt/<SID>/exe_new<ddmmyy>/*
/sapmnt/<SID>/exe/
```

8. This will copy / replace all the files in the existing kernel directory with a new kernel files.

9. Then check the kernel version from OS level by the command disp+work. It should show that the patch number has been increased.

10. Then logon to OS level as root (specific to UNIX). In the kernel directory, there is a script called saproot.sh. Execute this script

```
./saproot.sh <SID>
```

11. This script assigns the correct permissions to all the executable programs in the kernel such br* file etc...

12. Then start the SAP system

```
startsap r3
```

13. Now you can also check the kernel version level from SM51 or by selecting system > status

How to monitor SAP system and do performance checks

Why Daily Basic checks / System Monitoring?

Efficient Processing of Business	System Security and Stability	Avoid system issue on pro-active basis
FIRST	SECOND	THIRD

What is System Monitoring?

System monitoring is a *daily routine activity* and this document provides a systematic step by step procedure for Server Monitoring. It gives an overview of technical aspects and concepts for proactive system monitoring. Few of them are:

- Checking Application Servers.
- Monitoring System wide Work Processes.
- Monitoring Work Processes for Individual Instances.
- Monitoring Lock Entries.
- CPU Utilization
- Available Space in Database.
- Monitoring Update Processes.
- Monitoring System Log.
- Buffer Statistics

Some others are:

- Monitoring Batch Jobs
- Spool Request Monitoring.
- Number of Print Requests
- ABAP Dump Analysis.
- Database Performance Monitor.

- Database Check.
- Monitoring Application Users.

How do we do monitor a SAP System?

Checking Application Servers (SM51)

This transaction is used to check all active application servers.

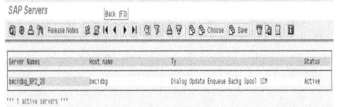

Here you can see which services or work processes are configured in each instance.

Monitoring Work Processes for Individual Instances SM50:

Displays all running, waiting, stopped and PRIV processes related to an instance. Under this step we check all the processes; the *process status should always be waiting or running*. If any process is having status other than waiting or running, we need to check that process and report accordingly.

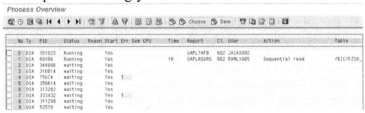

This transaction displays lot of information like:
1. Status of Work process (whether its occupied or not)
2. If the work process is running, you may be able to see the action taken by it in Action column.
3. You can which table is being worked upon

Some of typical problems:

- User take long time to log on/not able to logon/online transaction very slow. This could be the result of the DIA work processes are fully utilized. There could be also the result of long running jobs (red indicator under the Time column). If necessary, you can cancel the session by selecting the jobs then go to Process>Cancel Without core. This will cancel the job and release the work process for other user/process
- Some users may have PRIV status under **Reason** column. This could be that the user transaction is so big that it requires more memory. When this happen the DIA work process will be 'owned' by the user and will not let other users to use. If this happens, check with the user and if possible run the job as a background job.
- If there is a long print job on SPO work process, investigate the problem. It could be a problem related to the print server or printer.

Monitoring System Wide Work Processes (SM66)

By checking the work process load using the global work process overview, we can quickly investigate the potential cause of a system performance problem.

Monitor the work process load on all active instances **across the system**

Using the *Global Work Process Overview* screen, we can see at a glance:
- The status of each application server
- The reason why it is not running
- Whether it has been restarted

- The CPU and request run time
- The user who has logged on and the client that they logged on to
- The report that is running

Monitor Application User (AL08 and SM04)

This transaction displays all the users of active instances.

Monitoring Update Processes (SM13)

Execute Transaction SM13 and put '*' in the field USER and click on  button.

If there are no long pending updates records or no updates are going on than this queue will be empty as shown in the below screen shot.

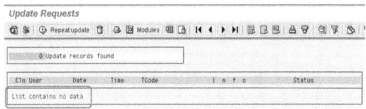

But, if the Update is not active then find the below information:

- Is the update active, if not, was it deactivated by system or by user?
    - Click on [Administration] button and get the information.
    - Click on button and get the below information:
- Is any update cancelled?

- Is there a long queue of pending updates older than 10 minutes?

Monitoring Lock Entries (SM12)

Execute Transaction SM12 and put '*' in the field User Name

SAP provides a *locking mechanism* to prevent other users from changing the record that you are working on. In some situations, locks are not released. This could happen if the users are cut off i.e. due to network problem before they are able to release the lock.

These old locks need to be cleared or it could prevent access or changes to the records.

We can use lock statistics to monitor the locks that are set in the system. We record only those lock entries which are having date time stamp of previous day.

Monitoring System Log (SM21)

We can use the log to pinpoint and rectify errors occurring in the system and its environment. We check log for the previous day with the following selection/option:

- Enter Date and time.
- Select Radio Button Problems and Warnings
- Press Reread System Log.

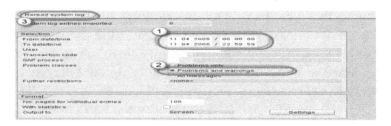

Tune Summary (ST02)

Step 1: Go to ST02 to check the Tune summary.

Step 2: If you see any red values, in SWAPS, double –click the same.

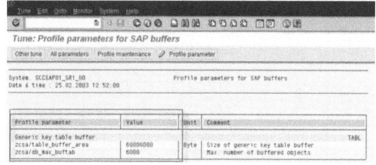

Step 3: In the below screen click on the tab '*Current Parameters*'

Step 4: Note down the *value* and the *Profile parameters*

Step 5: Go to RZ10 (to change the Profile parameter values)
Step 6: Save the changes.
Step 7: Restart the server to take the new changes effect.

CPU Utilization (ST06)

Local (bwcidbg) / Operating System Monitor: AIX

Refresh display   Detail analysis menu   Operating System collector

Wed Sep 7 11:35:29 2005   interval 10   sec.

CPU				
Utilization user %	2	Count		6
system %	13	CPU utilization 1 min		0,00
idle %	85	5 min		0,00
io wait %	0	15 min		0,00
System calls/s	57.031	Context switches/s		1.313
Interrupts/s	0			

Number of CPUs (→ Count line)

Should not go below 20% (→ idle/io wait lines)

Memory				
Physical mem avail Kb	12.582.764	Physical mem free Kb		27.460
Pages in/s	0	Kb paged in/s		0
Pages out/s	0	Kb paged out/s		0

Swap				
Configured swap Kb	35.979.264	Maximum swap-space Kb		35.979.264
Free in swap-space Kb	24.036.688	Actual swap-space Kb		35.979.264

Disk with highest response time				
Name	hdisk0	Response time ms		N/A
Utilization	2	Queue		N/A
Avg wait time ms	N/A	Avg service time ms		N/A
Kb transfered/s	25	Operations/s		5

LAN (sum)				
Packets in/s	21	Errors in/s		0
Packets out/s	22	Errors out/s		0
Collisions	0			

OS level commands –top

Idle CPU utilization rate must be 60-65%, if it exceeds the value then we must start checking at least below things:

- Run OS level commands – top and check which processes are taking most resources.
- Go to SM50 or SM66. Check for any long running jobs or any long update queries being run.
- Go to SM12 and check lock entries
- Go to SM13 and check Update active status.
- Check for the errors in SM21.

ABAP Dumps (ST22)

Here we check for previous day's dumps

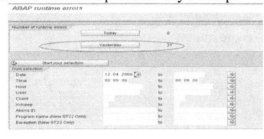

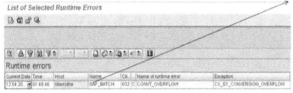

Open the details log of each and every dump by double clicking it and try to find out any suitable notes, analyze them and propose suitable solution as per SAP standards.

Spool Request Monitoring (SP01)

For spool request monitoring, execute SP01 and select as below:
- Put '*' in the field *Created By*
- Click on ⏻execute button.

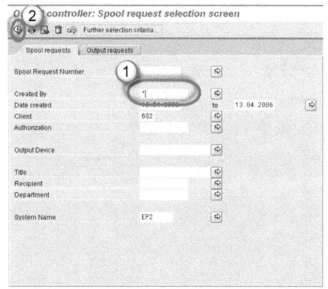

Here we record only those requests which are terminated with problems.

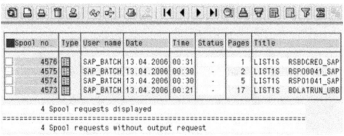

Monitoring Batch Jobs (SM37)

For Monitoring background jobs, execute SM37 and select as below:

- Put '*' in the field *User Name* and *Job name*
- In Job status, select: Scheduled, Cancelled, Released and Finished requests.

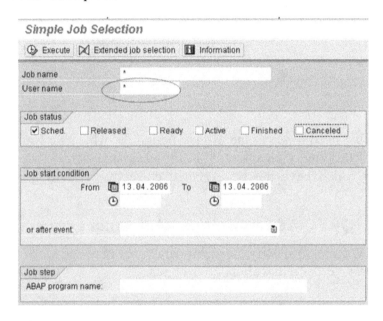

Transactional RFC Administration (SM58)

Transactional RFC (tRFC, also originally known as asynchronous RFC) is an asynchronous communication method which executes the called function module in the RFC server only once.

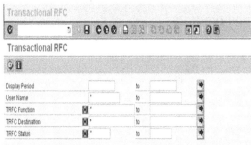

We need to select the display period for which we want to view the tRFCs and then select '*' in the username field to view all the calls which have not be executed correctly or waiting in queue.

QRFC Administration (Outbound Queue-SMQ1)

We should specify the client name over here and see if there any outgoing qRFCs in waiting or error state.

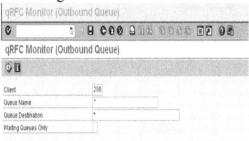

QRFC Administration (Inbound Queue -SMQ2)

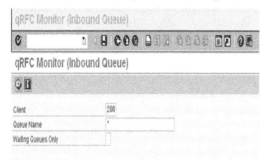

We should specify the client name over here and see if there any incoming qRFCs in waiting or error state.

Database Administration (DB02)

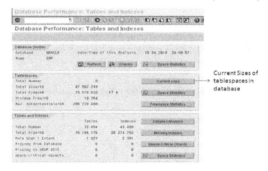

After you select **Current Sizes** on the first screen we come to the below screen which shows us the status of all the tablespaces in the system.

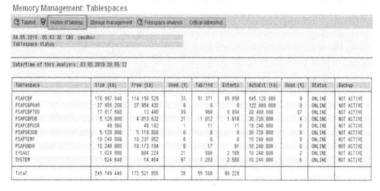

If any of the tablespace is more than 95% and the auto extent is off, then we need to add a new datafile so that the database is not full.

We can also determine the history of tablespaces.

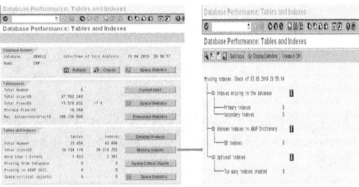

Tablespace History

Scale: Day	Size (Kbyte)		Free(Kbyte)	Used (Kbyte)		%-Used		Tables/Indices		Extents	
Tablespace	Total	Chg/day	Total	Total	Chg/day	Total	Chg	Total	Chg/day	Total	Chg/day
SYSAUX	1.824.000	0	804.224	219.776	400	21	0	986	1	2.188	6
PSAPUNDO	10.240.000	0	10.173.184	66.816	1.874	0	0	17	0	91	2
PSAPCBP	170.967.040	0	114.150.528	56.816.512	512	33	0	51.371	0	85.858	1

We can select Months, Weeks or Days over here to see the changes which takes place in a tablespace.

We can determine the growth of tablespace by analyzing these values.

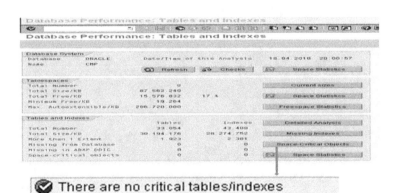

Database Backup logs (DB12)

From this transaction, we could determine when the last successful backup of the system was. We can review the previous day's backups and see if everything was fine or not.

We can also review the redo log files and see whether redo log backup was successful or not.

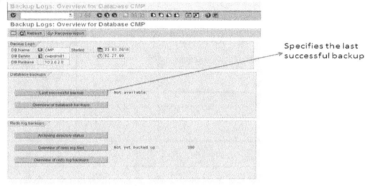

Quick Review

Daily Monitoring Tasks
1. Critical tasks
2. SAP System
3. Database

Critical tasks

o	Task	Transaction	Procedure / Remark
	Check that the R/3System is up.		Log onto the R/3 System
	Check that daily backups executed without errors	DB12	Check database backup.

SAP System

o	Task	Transaction	Procedure / Remark
	Check that all application servers are up.	SM51	Check that all servers are up.
	Check work processes (started from SM51).	SM50	All work processes with a "running" or a "waiting" status
	Global Work Process overview	SM66	Check no work process is running more than 1800 second
	Look for any failed updates (update terminates).	SM13	• Set date to one day ago • Enter * in the user ID • Set to "all" updates Check for lines with "Err."
	Check system log.	SM21	Set date and time to before the last log review. Check for:

	Task	Transaction	Procedure / Remark
			• Errors • Warnings • Security messages • Database problems
	Review for cancelled jobs.	SM37	Enter an asterisk (*) in User ID. Verify that all critical jobs were successful.
	Check for "old" locks.	SM12	Enter an asterisk (*) for the user ID.
	Check for users on the system.	SM04A L08	Review for an unknown or different user ID and terminal. This task should be done several times a day.
	Check for spool problems.	SP01	Enter an asterisk (*) for Created ByLook for spool jobs that have been "In process" for over an hour.
0	Check job log	SM37	Check for: • New jobs • Incorrect jobs
1	Review and resolve dumps.	ST22	Look for an excessive number of dumps. Look for dumps of an unusual nature.
2	Review buffer statistics.	ST02	Look for swaps.

Database

	Task	Transaction	Procedure / Remark
o			

Review error log for problems.	ST04	
Database GrowthMissing Indexes	DB02	If tablespace is used more than 90 % add new data file to it. Rebuild the Missing Indexes
Database Statistics log	DB13	

How to trace if an OSS Note is deployed in your landscape

SAP frequently releases "**Online SAP Support**" (**OSS**) Notes which may contain bug fixes, new program developments or enhancements or other miscellaneous updates.

At times before you begin work; it will be required to check whether a particular note is present in your SAP system

To ensure that a particular OSS note is present in your SAP system, execute the following steps:

1. In SAP command prompt, Enter TCode: SNOTE

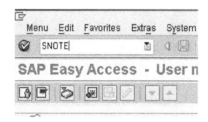

2. In the next screen, Click SAP Note Browser

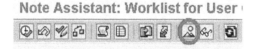

3. Type in your SAP Note Number in the corresponding text field and click execute

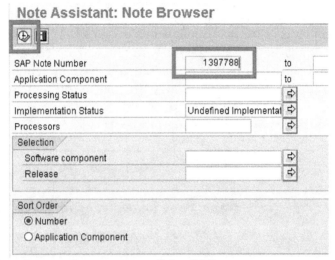

4. Next Screen shows status of the SAP note

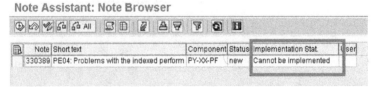

For a background, a SAP note could have any of the following seven status:

- Can be implemented
- Cannot be implemented
- Completely implemented
- Incompletely implemented
- Obsolete
- Obsolete version implemented
- Undefined Implementation State

Chapter 8. RFC

Introduction to RFC (Remote Function Call)

What is RFC?

For business applications, it is necessary to communicate and exchange information (in pre-defined formats) with other systems. Hence, there are well defined mechanisms to enable this communication. SAP has also provided us with such mechanism called **RFC**, which stands for **'Remote Function Call'**.

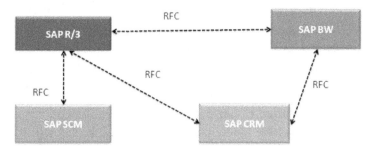

RFC is a SAP protocol to handle communications between systems to simplify the related programming. It is the process of calling a function module which is residing in a different machine from the caller program. RFCs can be used to call a different program in the same machine as well, but usually it is used when *'calling'* and *'called'* function modules/ programs are running on separate machines.

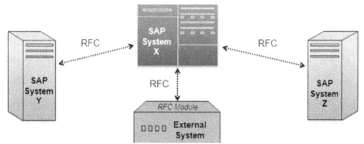

In SAP, RFC Interface system is used for setting-up RFC connections between different SAP systems, and between an SAP and an external (non-SAP) system.

Must Know Details about RFC

- SAP Uses CPIC (Common Programming Interface for Communication) Protocol to transfer data between Systems. It is SAP Specific protocol. Remote Function Call (RFC) is a communications interface based on CPI-C, but with more functions and easier for application programmers to use
- The RFC library functions support the C programming language and Visual Basic (on Windows platforms)
- RFC connections can always be used across the entire system. This means that an RFC connection you have defined in client 000 can also be used from client 100 (without any difference).
- RFC is the protocol for calling special subroutines (*function modules*) over the network. Function modules are comparable with C functions or PASCAL procedures. They have a defined interface through which data, tables and return codes can be exchanged. Function modules are managed in the R/3 System in their own function library, called the Function Builder.
- The Function Builder (transaction SM37) provides application programmers with a useful environment for programming, documenting and testing function modules that can be called locally as well as remotely. The R/3 System automatically generates the additional code (RFC stub) needed for remote calls.
- You maintain the parameters for RFC connections using transaction SM59. The R/3 System is also delivered with an RFC-SDK (Software Development Kit) that uses extensive C libraries to allow external programs to be connected to the R/3 System.
- The only difference between a remote call of a function module to another server and a local call is a special

parameter (destination) that specifies the target server on which the program is to be executed.

The RFC Advantages

RFC helps to reduce the efforts of programmers, by letting them avoid the re-development of modules and methods at remote systems. It is capable enough to:

- Convert the data into the format understandable by the remote (target) system.
- Convert the data into the format understandable by the remote (target) system.
- Call up certain routines which are necessary to start communication with remote system.
- Handle errors that might occur in the process of communication.

Types of RFC

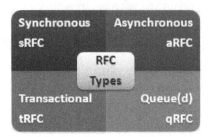

Synchronous

It requires both the systems (client and server) to be available at the time of communication or data transfer. It is the most common type and is required when result is required immediately after the execution of sRFC.

sRFC is a means of communication between systems where acknowledgements are required. The resources of the Source System wait at the target system and ensure that they deliver the message/data with ACKD. The Data is consistent and reliable for communication.

The issue is if the target system is not available, the source system resources wait until target system is available. This may lead to the Processes of source system to go into Sleep/RFC/CPIC Mode at target systems and hence blocks these resources.

Used for:
- For communication between systems
- For communication between SAP Web Application Server to SAP GUI

Asynchronous

It is communication between systems where acknowledgements are not required (it is similar to post card delivery). It doesn't require both the systems to be available at the time of execution and the result is not immediately required to be sent back to calling system.

The Source System resource does not wait for the target system as they deliver the message/data without waiting for any acknowledgement. It is not reliable for communication since data may be lost if the target system is not available.

Used for:
- For communication between systems
- For parallel processing

Transactional

It is a special form of aRFC. Transactional RFC ensures transaction-like handling of processing steps that were originally autonomous.

Transactional RFC is an asynchronous communication method that executes the called function module in the RFC server only once, even if the data is sent multiple times due to some network issue. The remote system need not be available at the time when the RFC client program is executing a tRFC. The tRFC component stores the called RFC function, together with the corresponding data, in the SAP database under a unique transaction ID (TID). tRFC is similar to aRFC as it does not wait at the target system (Similar to a registered post). If the system is not available, it will write the Data into aRFC Tables with a transaction ID (SM58) which is picked by the scheduler RSARFCSE (which runs for every 60 seconds).

Used for:
- Extension of Asynchronous RFC
- For secure communication between systems

Queued

Queued RFC is an extension of tRFC. It also ensures that individual steps are processed in sequence.

To guarantee that multiple LUWs (Logical Unit of Work/ Transaction) are processed in the order specified by the application. tRFC can be serialized using queues (inbound and outbound queues). Hence the name queued RFC (qRFC).

Used for:
- *Extension of the Transactional RFC*
- *For a defined processing sequence*

- Implementation of qRFC is recommended if you want to guarantee that several transactions are processed in a predefined order.

Types of RFC Connections – SM59

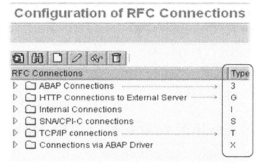

Type 3 - entries specify connection between ABAP systems. Here, we must specify the host name / IP address. You can, however, specify logon information if desired. This is applicable for both type of RFCs, between ABAP systems and external calls to ABAP systems

Type I - entries specify ABAP systems connected to the same data base as the current system. These entries are pre-defined and cannot be modified. Example entry name: ws0015_K18_24

- ws0015=host name
- K18=system name (data base name)
- 24=TCP-service name

Type T - destinations are connections to external programs that use the RFC API to receive RFCs. The activation type can be either *Start* or *Registration*. If it is *Start*, you must specify the host name and the pathname of the program to be started.

How to Configure and Test RFC.

This tutorial is divided into 4 sections
1. Setup a RFC connection
2. Trusted RFC connection
3. Testing a RFC connection
4. Error Resolution

Procedure to setup an RFC connection:

Enter Transaction Code **SM59**

In the SM59 screen, you can navigate through already created RFCs connection with the help of option tree, which is a menu based method to organize all the connections based on categories.

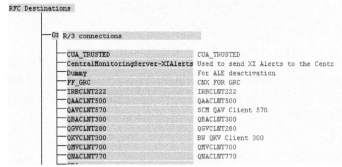

Click the '*CREATE*' button. In the next screen, Enter:
- **RFC Destination** – Name of Destination (could be Target System ID or anything relevant)
- **Connection Type** – here we choose one of the types (as explained previously) of RFC connections as per requirements.
- **Description** – This is a short informative description, probably to explain the purpose of connection.

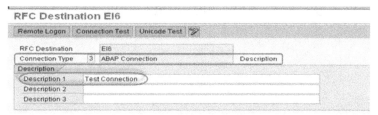

After you 'SAVE' the connection, the system will take you to 'Technical Settings' tab, where we provide the following information:

- **Target Host**– Here we provide the complete hostname or IP address of the target system.
- **System Number** – This is the system number of the target SAP system.
- Click Save

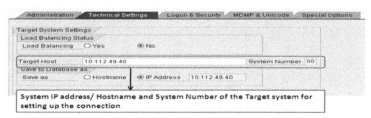

In the **'Logon and Security'** Tab, Enter Target System information

- **Language** – As per the target system's language
- **Client** – In SAP we never logon to a system, there should be a client always, therefore we need to specify client number here for correct execution.
- **User ID and Password** – preferably not to be your own login ID, there should be some generic ID so that the connection should not be affected by constantly changing end-user IDs or passwords. *Mostly, a user of type 'System' or 'Communication' is used here.* Please note that this is the User ID for the target system and not the source system where we are creating this connection.

- Click Save. RFC connection is ready for use

Note: By default, a connection is defined as aRFC. To define a connection as tRFC or qRFC go to Menu Bar -> Destination aRFC options / tRFC options; provide inputs as per requirements. To define qRFC, use the special options tab.

Trusted RFC connection

There is an option to make the RFC connection as 'Trusted'. Once selected, the calling (trusted) system doesn't require a password to connect with target (trusting) system.

Following are the advantages for using trusted channels:

- Cross-system Single-Sign-On facility
- Password does not need to be sent across the network
- Timeout mechanism for the logon data prevents misuse.
- Prevents the mishandling of logon data because of the time-out mechanism.
- User-specific logon details of the calling/trusted system are checked.

The RFC users must have the required authorizations in the trusting system (authorization object S_RFCACL). Trusted connections are mostly used to connect SAP Solution Manager Systems with other SAP systems (satellites)

Testing the RFC Connection

After the RFCs are created (or sometimes in case of already existing RFCs) we need to test, whether the connection is established successfully or not.

As shown above we go to SM59 to choose the RFC connection to be tested and then we expand drop down menu - **"Utilities->Test->..."**. We have three options:

Connection test -> This attempts to make a connection with remote system and hence validates IP address / Hostname and other connection details. If both systems are not able to connect, it throws an error. On success, it displays the table with response times. This test is just to check if the calling system is able to reach the remote system.

Authorization Test -> It is used to validate the User ID and Password (provided under 'logon and security' tab for the target system) and the authorizations that are provided. If test is successful, then same screen will appear as shown above for the connection test.

Unicode Test -> It is to check if the Target system is a Unicode or not.

Remote Logon –>This is also a kind of connection test, in which a new session of the target system is opened, and we need to specify a login ID and Password (if not already mentioned under 'Logon and Security' tab). If the user is of type 'Dialog' then a dialog session is created. To justify the successful connection test, output will be the response times for the communication packets, else error message will appear.

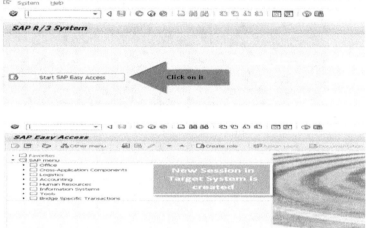

What went wrong?

If somehow the RFC connection is not established successfully, we can check the logs (to analyze the issue) at OS level in the 'WORK' director. There we can find the log files with the naming convention as "*dev_rfc <sequence no.>*" and the error description can be read from such files.

```
cwprdm01:cmpadm 10> pwd
/usr/sap/CMP/DVEBMGS00/work
```

```
cwprdm01:cmpadm 11> more dev_rfc1
**** Trace file opened at 20100415 203854 EST SAP-REL 701,0,59 RFC-VER 0 3 1093028
=====> CPIC-CALL: 'ThSAPOCMINIT' : cmRc=2 thRc=679
Transaction program not registered
ABAP Programm: CL_SLD_ACCESSOR=============CP (Transaction: )
User: RYANK (Client: 000)
Destination: SAPJ2EE (handle: 1, , )
Error RFCIO_ERROR_SYSERROR in abrfcpic.c : 1501
CPIC-CALL: 'ThSAPOCMINIT' : cmRc=2 thRc=679
Transaction program not registered
DEST =SAPJ2EE
HOST =%%RFCSERVER%%
PROG =sapfallback
GWHOST =cwprdm01
GWSERV =sapgw00
=====> CPIC-CALL: 'ThSAPOCMINIT' : cmRc=2 thRc=679
Transaction program not registered
ABAP Programm: CL_SLD_ACCESSOR=============CP (Transaction: )
User: RYANK (Client: 000)
Destination: SAPJ2EE (handle: 2, , )
Error RFCIO_ERROR_SYSERROR in abrfcpic.c : 1501
CPIC-CALL: 'ThSAPOCMINIT' : cmRc=2 thRc=679
Transaction program not registered
DEST =SAPJ2EE
```

Path for 'Work' directory at OS level

Log File name

Error Description

Chapter 9. Data Migration

All about IDOC: Definition, Architecture, Implementation

What is an IDOC?

IDOC is simply a data container used to exchange information between any two processes that can understand the syntax and semantics of the data.

In other words, an IDOC is like a data file with a specified format which is exchanged between 2 systems which know how to interpret that data.

IDOC stands for "Intermediate Document"

When we execute an outbound ALE or EDI Process, an IDOC is created.

In the SAP System, IDOCs are stored in database. Every IDOC has a unique number (within a client).

Key Features

- IDOCs are independent of the sending and receiving systems. (SAP-to-SAP as well as Non-SAP)
- IDOCs are based on EDI standards, ANSI ASC X12 and EDIFACT. In case of any conflict in data size, it adopts one with greater length.
- IDOCs are independent of the direction of data exchange e.g. ORDERS01: Purchasing module: Inbound and Outbound
- IDOCs can be viewed in a text editor. Data is stored in character format instead of binary format.

Structure of an IDOC

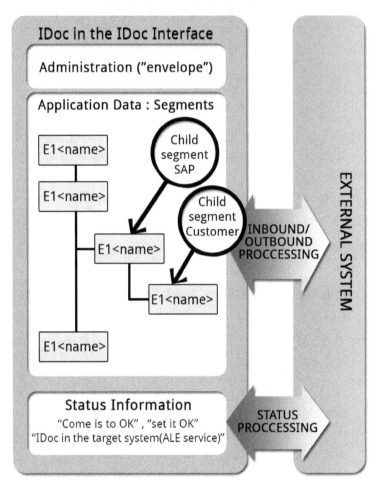

The Idoc structure consists of 3 parts:

1. The administration part (**Control Record**)- which has the type of idoc, message type, the status, the sender, receiver etc. This is referred to as the Control record.
2. The application data (**Data Record**) - Which contains the data. These are called the data records/*segments*.
3. The Status information (**Status Record**)- These give you information about the various stages the idoc has passed through.

You can view an IDOC using transaction WE02 or WE05

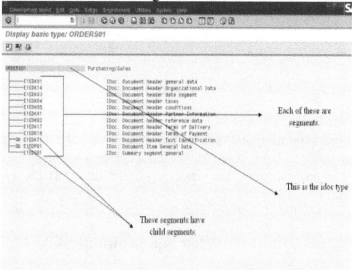

As seen in screenshot above IDOC record has three parts Control, Data and Status. Let's consider them in detail - **Control Record**

- All control record data is stored in EDIDC table. The key to this table is the IDOC Number
- It contains information like IDOC number, the direction (inbound/outbound), sender, recipient information, channel it is using, which port it is using etc.
- Direction '1' indicates outbound, '2' indicates inbound.

Data Record

- Data record contains application data like employee header info, weekly details, client details etc.
- All data record data is stored in EDID2 to EDID4 tables and EDIDD is a structure where you can see its components.
- It contains data like the idoc number, name and number of the segment in the idoc, the hierarchy and the data
- The actual data is stored as a string in a field called SDATA, which is a 1000 char long field.

Status Record

- Status records are attached to an IDOC at every milestone or when it encounters errors.
- All status record data is stored in EDIDS table.
- Statuses 1-42 are for outbound while 50-75 for inbound

IDOC Types

An IDOC Type (Basic) defines the structure and format of the business document that is to be exchanged. **An IDOC is an instance of an IDOC Type,** just like the concept of variables and variables types in programming languages. You can define IDOC types using **WE30**

What is a Segment?

Segment defines the format and structure of a **data record** in IDOC. Segments are reusable components. For each segment SAP creates:
- Segment Type (version independent)
- Segment Definition (version dependent)
- Segment Documentation

The last 3 characters is the version of the segment
Definitions keep changing as per the version but the segment type remains the same.
Transaction: **WE31**

Development segments: Display segment definition E2EDKT1002

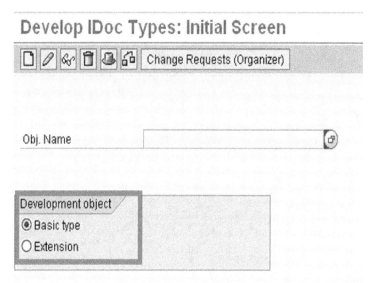

Po..	Field Name	Data element	ISO c.	Ex.
1	TDID	EDI4451_A		4
2	TSSPRAS	EDI3453_A		3
3	TSSPRAS_ISO	LAISO	✓	2
4	TDOBJECT	TDOBJECT		10
5	TDOBNAME	TDOBNAME		70

What is Extension IDOC type?

An IDOC is of 2 types:

1. Basic
2. Extension

SAP provides many a pre-defined Basic IDOC Types which **can not be modified**. In case you want to add more data to these restricted basic types you may use an extension type. Most of the times you will **NOT** use extension.

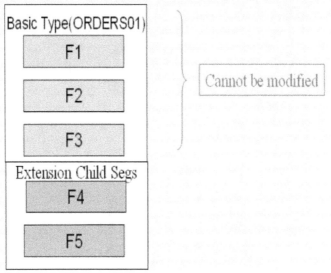

Documentation

Each IDOC are thoroughly documented in transaction **WE60**

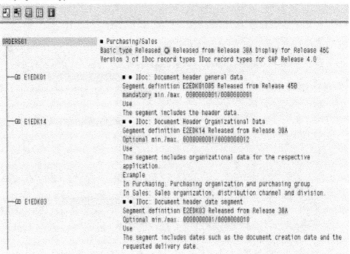

Message Type

A message represents a specific type of document that is transmitted between two partners Ex. Orders, orders responses, invoices etc.

An idoc type can be associated with many message types

Also, a message type can be associated with different idoc types. Transaction **WE81**

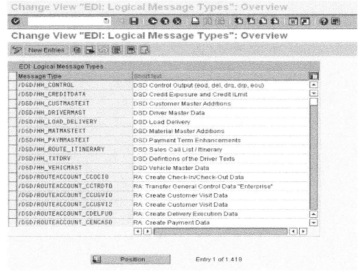

IDOC Views

An IDOC type can be used for more than one message type, which results in IDOCs containing more fields than required for a message type.

IDOC views are used to improve performance in generating IDOCs to ensure only the relevant segments are filled with data. IDOC Views are important only for Outbound Processing.

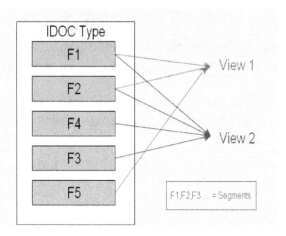

Partner Profiles

A partner is defined as a business partner with whom you conduct business and exchange documents.

In the partner profile of a partner that we exchange Idocs with, we maintain the parameters that are necessary for exchanging the data. The transaction used is **WE20**.

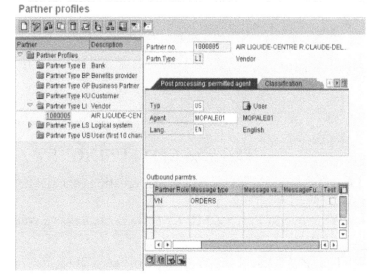

Port

The port defines the technical characteristics of the connection between your SAP system and the other system you want to transfer data with (subsystem). The port defines the medium in which data is exchanged between the 2 systems.

There are different types of ports. The 2 most commonly used are the **TRFC ports** used in ALE and **File** ports which EDI uses.

For TRFC ports we should give the name of the logical destination created using **SM59**.

When using file port, you can specify the directory where the IDOC file should be placed. The other system or the middleware will pick up the file from here. The Function module can be used to generate a file name for the idoc. While testing, you can use "Outbound file" to specify a constant file name. The tab "**outbound trigger**" can be used to supply information if we want to trigger some processing on the subsystem when an idoc is created at this location. We have to specify the command file name and the directory which has to be run.

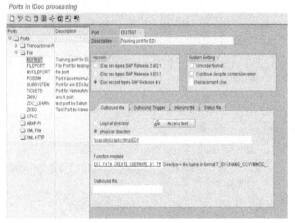

Ports in IDoc processing

This is so CONFUSING!

Let's understand the process of creating an IDOC with an example:

- Whenever a Purchase Order (PO) is created we want to send the IDOC to a vendor.
- The PO is sent in the form of an IDOC to the vendor (partner). That partner has to be EDI enabled in that system. SAP should realize that it could send doc to this vendor electronically.
- The PO sent as an outbound idoc by the customer will be inbound idoc for the vendor. The SAP system on the vendor's side can process this to create an application document (a sales order) on their system.
- Quotation, RFQ, PO, SO, Invoice, delivery note etc. are some of the commonly exchanged documents through IDOC

The process of data transfer out of your SAP system is called the **Outbound process**, while that of data moving into you SAP system is called **Inbound process**. As a developer or a consultant who will be involved in setting up theses process for your organization. Here are the steps how to set them up.

The Outbound Process

Steps Involved:
1. Create segments (WE31)
2. Create an idoc type (WE30)
3. Create a message type (WE81)
4. Associate a message type to idoc type (WE82)
5. Create a port (WE21)
6. If you are going to use the message control method to trigger idocs then create the function module for creating the idoc and associate the function module to an outbound process code
7. Otherwise create the function module or standalone program which will create the idoc
8. Create a partner profile (WE20) with the necessary information in the outbound parameters for the partner you want to exchange the idoc with Trigger the idoc.

The Inbound Process

Steps Involved:
1. Creation of basic Idoc type (Transaction WE30)
2. Creating message type (Transaction WE81)
3. Associating the Message type to basic Idoc type (Transaction WE82)
4. Create the function module for processing the idoc
5. Define the function module characteristics (BD51)
6. Allocate the inbound function module to the message type(WE57)
7. Defining process code (Transaction WE42)
8. Creation of partner profile (Transaction WE20)

What is SAP LSMW?

The **LSMW** Workbench is a tool that **supports the transfer of data from non-SAP systems ("Legacy Systems") to SAP R/3 systems**. This can be a one-time transfer as well as a periodic one.

LSMW also supports **conversion of data** of the legacy system in numerous ways. The data can then be imported into the SAP R/3 system via **batch input, direct input, BAPIs or IDocs**.

Furthermore, the LSM Workbench provides a recording function that allows generating a "**data migration object**" to enable migration from any required transaction.

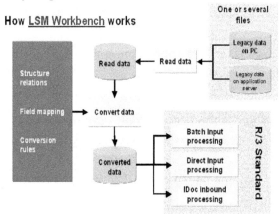

LSMW can be used for following **3 functions**:
The main functions of the LSM Workbench are:

1. **Import data** (legacy data in spreadsheet tables and/or sequential files)
2. **Convert data** (from source format to target format)
3. **Import data** (into the database of the R/3 application)

To start the LSMW workbench use transaction **LSMW**

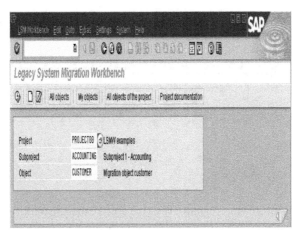

Also, check out next tutorial on executing LSMW Step by Step

How to Migrate Data using LSMW

Enter Transaction **LSMW** in SAP, to start the workbench.

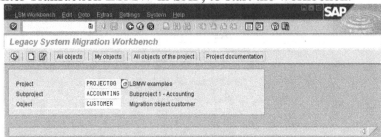

LSMW workbench shows the following information:

- **Project**: An ID with a maximum of 10 characters to name your data transfer project. If you want to transfer data from several legacy systems, you may create a project e.g. for every legacy system.

- **Subproject**: An ID with a maximum of 10 characters that is used as a further structuring attribute.

- **Object**: An ID with a maximum of 10 characters to name the business object.

Enter Project ID, Subproject ID, Object ID. Click Execute The next screen gives the **STEPS** in your LSMW data Migration

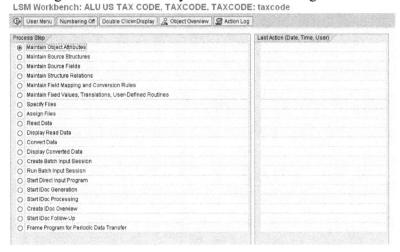

You can select a desired step and click execute. Let's consider each step-in detail

Step 1 - Maintain Object Attributes.

```
Attributes
  Object            CUSTOMERS  Customer master ( BI )
  Owner             OHLIGER        OHLIGER
  Data transfer     ● once                  ○ periodic
  File names        □ system dependent

Object type and import technique
  ● Standard Batch/Direct Input
    Object            0050   Customer master
    Method            0000
    Program name      RFBIDE00
    Program type      B    Batch input
  ○ Batch Input Recording
    Recording
  ○ Business Object Method (BAPI)
    Business object
    Method
    Message type
    Basic type
  ○ IDoc (Intermediate Document)
    Message type
    Basic type
    Enhancement
```

There are **four Modes of Data Transfer**:

1. **Standard/ Batch Input**: Standard upload Programs
2. **Batch Input Recording**: Here you can create a recording of your own and use it to upload / change data
3. **BAPIs:** Standard BAPIs are used to upload Data
4. **IDOCs:** Any Inbound IDOC function modules can be used to process the data

Based on the requirement we try to find a suitable method to be processed. If it is a standard Master we can find it in the first method, otherwise we try to use BAPIs or Idocs. If the requirement is a very custom one, we use a recording to process the data.

Step 2 - Maintain Source Structures

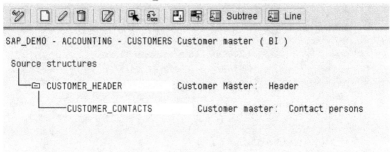

The source structures can be used to design the hierarchy of the files to be uploaded.

Step 3 - Maintain Source Fields

In this screen, the Fields which will be uploaded from the text file can be maintained here. The fields with identical names are taken as the Key

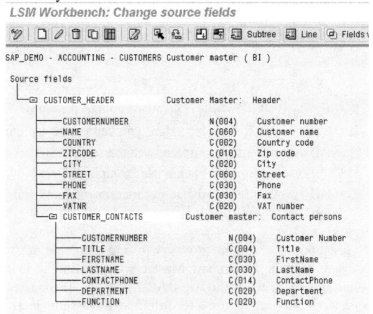

Source Filed is used to identify whether a certain record should go to the specified structure. E.g.: Suppose a file contains header

rows and item rows, we can specify the first field as the indicator say 'H' for header and 'I' for Item. Thus, when the file is being read, it checks the first field, if it is 'H' then it is read into the Header source structure else it is written to the item source structure.

The Source fields can be easily maintained in the form of table maintenance.

Step 4 - Maintain Structure Relationships

The Structures which are needed for the processing of the data need to be assigned here. The Object may contain many structures and many source structures. The Mapping between the source and the target structures should be done after careful checking.

Step 5 - Maintain Field Mapping and Conversion Rules

In this step, you assign source fields to target fields and define how the field contents will be converted.

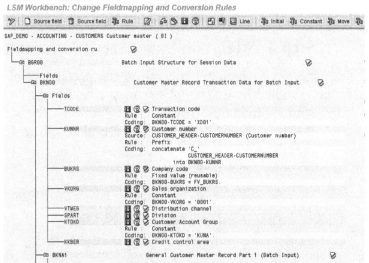

All fields of all target structures, which you selected in the previous step, will be displayed. For each target field the following information is displayed:

- Field description
- Assigned source fields (if any)
- Rule type (fixed value, translation etc.)
- Coding.

Note: Some fields are preset by the system. These fields are called "technical fields" are marked with "Default setting". The coding for these fields is not displayed when first entering the field mapping; it can be displayed via the display variant. Changing the default setting may seriously affect the flow of the data conversion. If you erroneously changed the default setting, you can restore it by choosing Extras -> Restore default.

Step 6 - Maintain Fixed Values, Translations and User-written Routines

Here the 3 reusable functions are maintained:

---

1. **Fixed Values**: Fixed values are values which are fixed across the project e.g.: Company Code. We can assign a fixed value to BUKRS and this fixed value can be used in all the objects in this project. So, if the value changes we can only change at one place i.e. in the fixed values instead of changing in each object.

2. **Translations**: Here you can maintain the fixed translation for any legacy field and the translation can be assigned to the filed in Field Mapping and Conversion Rules. Translation can be 1:1 or many: 1 etc.

3. **User Defined Routines**: These are user defined subroutines that are used in the object for processing the data.

All the Three functions mentioned above are reusable Rules which are valid for all objects in one Project.

Step 7 - Specify Files

Here we define the Files that we use to upload the data. The File can be on the Front end or in the application server.

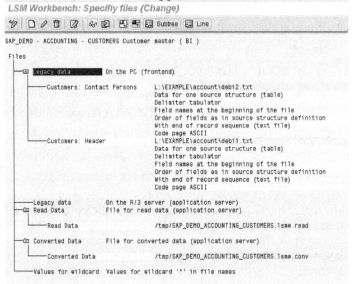

Step 8 - Assign Files

Here we define which file we are going to use for current upload i.e. whether the file is on Presentation server or application server.

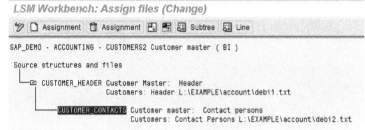

Step 9 - Read Data

Reading the data from the file gives us an option to read only a few records and not the entire chunk to enable testing of first few records. This also provides the user defined selection parameter which can be used to restrict the read data based on the condition specified.

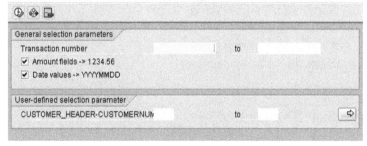

Step 10 - Display Read Data

- In this step, you can display all or a part of the read data in table form. Clicking on a line displays all information for this line in a clear way. The same happens when you click on Field contents.
- Change display allows to select either a one-line or multi-line view.
- Display color palette displays the colors for the individual hierarchy levels.

Step 11 - Convert Data

Converting the data is the transfer of data from source to target structures based on the conversion routines written in maintain Field Mapping and conversion routines.

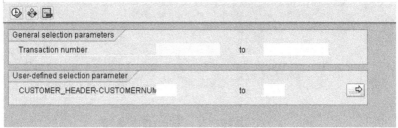

Step 12- Import Data

The steps displayed by the program depend on the selected object type:

Standard batch input or recording:
1. Generate batch input session
2. Run batch input session

Standard direct input:
1. Start direct input session

BAPI or IDoc:
1. Start IDoc creation
2. Start IDoc processing
3. Create IDoc overview
4. Start IDoc post processing

This completes a detailed overview of steps to transfer your data using LSMW in SAP.

Chapter 10. SAP Basis Interview Question

1) What is SAP Basis?

SAP basis acts as an operating system or a platform for SAP applications to run. It supports the entire range of SAP applications.

2) What is the difference between Developer Trace, System Log and System Trace?

a) System Trace: When you want to record internal SAP system activities, system trace is used. The trace is useful in diagnosis internal problems within SAP system and the host system.

b) System Log: To know the recent logs for application server and CI, System log is referred.

c) Developer Trace: In the event of problems, developer trace, records the technical information about the error or problem

For problem analysis and system monitoring Developer trace or System log is used.

3) In a situation where My SAP system is down (Users unable to login to SAP system), how to analyze the problem?

a) Check the Database status

b) SAP services

c) SAP management console (Dispatcher, IGS and Message Server)

d) You need to find out trace root based on point at serial no (c).

e) Check network connectivity if everything is ok

4) What is private mode?

In private mode, the heap data is exclusively allocated by the user and is no more shared or available across the system. This occurs when your extended memory is exhausted.

5) What is OSP$ mean?

Two users "OPS$adm" and "OPS$SAP" Service are created in your SAP system and to connect and communicate with database internally this user mechanism is used.

6) What are the different types of RFC and explain what Transactional RFC is?

RFC (Remote Function Call) is a mechanism to communicate and exchanging the information between other SAP systems. There are four types of RFC's system

a) Synchronous RFC (S RFC)
b) Asynchronous RFC (A RFC)
c) Transactional RFC (T RFC)
d) Queued RFC (Q RFC)

Transactional RFC (T RFC): This type of RFC is similar to asynchronous RFC, but by allocating a transaction ID (TID) it makes sure that the request sent multiple times due to an error must process only for once. In T RFC, the remote system does not have to be available at the moment unlike asynchronous RFC.

7) What is OCM and how to apply OCM Patches?

OCM stands for online correction system; by using SPAM you can apply OCM Patches.

8) How to perform a SAP-export and import tables in SAP from OS level?

To export or import tables in SAP from OS level you have to follow three steps and by using R3trans utility in SAP

Step 1: Collect all lists of tables to be exported

Step 2: Check whether enough disk space is available in the directory where you going to export.

Step 3: Create two control files for R3trans which will be used for import and export.

9) What is the difference between – support package, kernel and SAP note?

SAP Note: An error in a single transaction or program is removed by implementing a SAP note.

Kernel: Kernel contains the executable files (.EXE) like other applications and when a Kernel upgrade is done a new version of the EXE file replaces the older versions.

Support Package: SAP support packages is a bunch of corrections; this can be used by applying transaction SPAM

10) How can you find the list of objects that have been repaired in the system?

The list of objects that have been repaired can be found in the system having ADIRACCESS keys.

11) What is the purpose of table TADIR?

Table TADIR contains object directory entries.

12) Is it possible to install SAP patches when other users are online?

When other users are online we can't install SAP patches, as support manager will not be able to update and it will terminate it. So, it is always feasible to better apply support packs when there is no user's login into the system.

13) Mention what is the difference between SDM and JSPM?

JSPM (Java Support Package Manager) is used to apply support packages on deployed software components. In other words, it's a tool that allows you to install the components and support packages.

SDM (Software Delivery Manager) is used for importing Java Support Packages. To deploy and manage software packages received from SAP, SDM tool is used.

JSPM uses SDM for the deployment purpose

14) What is the procedure to disable import all option from STMS in SAP?

To disable import all option from STMS in SAP, steps are:

a) Go to STMS T-code

b) Go to menu option overview

c) Select System

d) Choose SAP System

e) Go to transport tool tab

f) Create parameter "No_Import_All" with value set as 1

g) Save it

15) Mention the use of personalized tab and parameter tab in user master record?

Parameter Tab: It will allow access to assign T-code on which one has to work

Personalization Tab: It is required for RFC connection between systems other than user personal information

16) What is the different type of users in SAP?

Different types of users in SAP are

a) Dialog Users
b) System Users
c) Communication Users
d) Service Users
e) Reference Users

17) Explain what is the use of reference and service user in SAP?

- **Service User:** For "service user" initial password or expiration of password are not checked. Only admin has rights to change the password, users cannot. Multiple logins are possible.

Usage: Service users are for anonymous users. Minimum authorization should be given to such type of users

- **Reference User:** For this kind of user's GUI login is not possible.

Usage: In case of emergency, with the help of reference user, it is possible to provide one user authorization to another user.

18) Explain how you can restrict multiple logins of user in SAP? What are the things you have to take care of while writing the ID's?

To restrict multiple logins, you must set the parameter as
Parameter should set in RZ10

a) login/multi_login_users= set to 1 to activate (If this parameter is set to value 1, multiple dialog logons to the R/3 system are blocked)

b) login/disable_multi_gui_login= List out the users that should be allow to logon for multiple times

While writing the user ID's things to be taken care are, list the user IDs separated by commas "..", between user IDs do not leave space characters and to see the changes restart the R/3 instance.

19) At OS level how you can change the number of work process? How you can analyze the status of work process at OS level?

To change the number of work process at the OS level, you can increase the no. of work processes by modifying the parameter rdisp/wp_no_ =

Status of a WP at OS level can be checked by executing dpmon.

20) Explain how to define logon groups?

Logon groups can be defined using the T-Code smlg. To do that you should create the group and then assign the instances for that group.

21) What is SAP single stack system?

A single stack system is defined by SAP system either with JAVA as runtime engine or SAP NetWeaver as ABAP.

E.g.: Single Stack System (Java) is SAP Enterprise Portal System (Ep)

Single Stack System (ABAP) is SAP ERP (ECC)

22) What are the tools to install JAVA patches?

To use the JAVA patches, SAP installer (SAPinst.exe) is employed. SDM and JSPM are the latest versions of tools used to deploy Java Patches.

23) Explain what is "Data Sets" in SAP?

To solve queries which cannot be solved by using the method interfaces, a set of information is used. This set of information is known as "Data Sets".

24) At O.S level where to check for system logs of SAP application?

The system Logs of SAP Application at OS Level can be checked at SAPMMC > SAP Systems > SID > Syslog.

System logs can be checked in T-Code SM21, we can see the system logs at OS level usr/sap/sid/sys/logs directory

25) Explain what is LUW (logical unit of work)?

A list of steps among t-code in known as logical LUW

26) Explain what is heterogeneous system copy and homogenous system copy?

Homogenous system copy= Same OS + Same Database

Heterogeneous system copy= Different OS + Different database or same database

27) Explain what are the functional modules used in sequence in BDC?

Using BDC programming a data can be transferred successfully. There are 3 functional modules which can be used in a sequence.

a) **BDC _OPEN_GROUP**: Name of the client, sessions and user name are specified in these functional modules.

b) **BDC_INSERT**: It is used to insert the data for one transaction into a session.

c) **BDC_CLOSE_GROUP**: It is used to close the batch input session.

28) Explain what is an "OK" code is and what is the difference between "t-code" and "OK" code?

An "OK" code is used by a program to execute a function for example after a push button has been clicked.

Transaction code or "t-code" is a "shortcut" that helps a user to run a program.

29) Explain how client refresh is different than client copy?

Client refresh is overwriting or copying to existing client, while copying the newly created client is called client copy.

30) What is a background processing batch scheduler?

To check the schedule background jobs and to execute them parameters like rdisp/btctime is used. These parameters define background processing batch scheduler.

31) Explain what is SAP IDES?

SAP Internet Demonstration and Evaluation System or SAP IDES, this system demonstrate the functionality of various SAP solutions used by important customers.

32) Explain what is the purpose of TDEVC?

The purpose of TDEVC contains development classes and packages.

33) How many types of work processes are there in SAP?

There are seven types of work processes they are:

a) Dialog

b) Enque

c) Update

d) Background

e) Spool

f) Message

g) Server

h) Gateway

34) What is the role of "Application Server"?

Application Server takes the request from the user and if the request requires data then it connects to the database server and gives output.

35) What is process for applying patches?

Processes for applying patches are:

a) Download patches from the service.sap.com to Trans Directory

b) Using CAR command extract the patches in the Trans Directory

c) Using SAPM, import patches into SAP level and Apply

36) How to perform the transport?

Transport can be done through STMS_IMPORT or through FTP.

37) What are the types of transport queries?

a) Customizing Request

b) Workbench Request

c) Transport of Copies

d) Re-location

38) Explain what is business KPIs?

Business KPIs are Key Performance Indicators. It indicates the performance of a company at a strategic level. They help in leading the company on the desired track by comparing company's previous performance with the market leaders in the same market.

39) Explain what is the importance of table T000?

Table T000 contains a list of defined clients, where we can maintain transaction code SCC4.

40) What is SAPS?

SAPS stands for SAP Application Performance Standard, which is a hardware independent unit which describes the performance of a system configuration in SAP environment.

41) Mention what is the difference between Central Instance & Application Server?

Central Instance has message server and dialog, update, spool, enque, gateway, background work processes.

Application server has dialog, update, spool, gateway, and background work process.

42) In what ways you would know whether a system is Unicode or Non-Unicode?

By code sm51 t-code we can see whether it is Unicode or non-Unicode. In this code, we can find the release notes button in the application tool bar if you click on that you can see the total information like Database, Kernel version, Unicode or non-Unicode.

43) In SAP basis what are the different types of transport requests?

Four types of transport requests are there

a) Customizing request

b) Workbench request

c) Transport request

d) Relocation

44) What is logical system? How to create and why?

For communication between systems within the landscapes logical system is required. It enables the system to recognize the target system as an RFC destination.

TCODE used is SPRO

45) How you can assign an object to 100 roles at time?

To assign an object to 100 roles at time,

a) Go to sell T-code from there go to the table agr_agrs.

b) You will be asked for Access key

c) Enter the objects that needs to be added to 100 roles

d) Select the range of roles in which the object needs to be added

e) Save or activate whatever option is given

46) On a system how you can get a list of the users with development access on a particular system?

By using table "DEVACCESS" you can get a list of the users with development access.

47) How can you view locked transactions?

To view locked transactions, you need to look in field CINFO, table TSTC. Within SAP you can either use SE11 or SE16 to browse the table contents. Ensure that you enter "A0" as the "HEX01 data element for SYST" starting value and "A9" as the ending value. This will list all the transactions locked in the system.

48)   What is an 'OK' code? What are the differences an 'OK' code to a 'T-code'?

OK code is used by a program to execute a function for example after a pushbutton has been clicked. A transaction code is a "shortcut" that helps a user run program.

49)   How you can disable the 'Import All' button on STMS for the queues?

a) Login to your Transport Domain Controller

b) Run STMS > Overview > System

c) Choose the system you want to disable 'Import All'

d) Go to Transport Tool tab

e) Add/Create parameter "No_IMPORT_ALL" set its value to 1

50)   How you can apply SAP notes to SAP system?

a) Go to Tcode SNOTE

b) Go to Menu > Download SAPNote

c) Give the Note No

d) After downloading check the status, if implemented

e) Select Note, GOTO Menu SAPNote > Implement Note

51)   Mention what is the purpose of table USR02?

This table stores passwords and User IDS.

52)   What is the difference between kernel replacement and support package?

Kernel replacement is the replacement of the SAP executable on the OS level, while support package contains fixes to the ABAP code within a SAP instance.

53) Which are the most frequent errors encountered while dealing with TRANSPORTS?

Return code (4) indicates import ended with warning.

Return code (8) indicates not imported ended with error

Return code (12) indicates import is cancelled.

Return code (16) indicates import is cancelled.

54) How will go about doing a client copy?

You can do a client copy using the SCCL transaction

55) List the difference between asynchronous and synchronous transport!

Synchronous Transport - Dialog or batch process are blocked until import is ended

Asynchronous Transport - Dialog or batch process is released after import is started.

55) How will determine whether your SAP server is Unicode or ASCII?

Go to SM51, Click Release Notes. Entry corresponding to ICU Version will tell you whether your system is ASCII or Unicode.

56) List the types of Transport requests?

There are 4 types of transport requests in SAP -

1. Customizing Request
2. Workbench Request
3. Transport of Copies
4. Relocation

57) What is the difference between Consolidation and Development route?

In consolidation route - objects can be changed and they can transport from one system to other. This is the route between developments to quality

In Development route - Objects cannot be changed and they cannot be transported from one system to other. This is the route between qualities to production

58) How will you define logon groups? What is Load Balancing in SAP?

You can set the logon group using SMLG transaction.

59) What is supplementation language?

Default SAP systems are pre-installed with English and German.

SAP does support many other languages which may not full translate from the default English and German. To fill this gap, Supplementary language (a program) is installed.

60) Is SAP a database?

NO. SAP is not a database but it uses databases from other vendors like Oracle. Although SAP has recently released its own database HANA.

61) Which transaction do you use to check Buffer Statistics?
ST02, RZ10

---: FINISH: -

www.ingramcontent.com/pod-product-compliance
Lightning Source LLC
LaVergne TN
LVHW022310060326
832902LV00020B/3385